KIDS KILLING KIDS

Managing Violence and Gangs in Schools

KIDS KILLING KIDS

Managing Violence and Gangs in Schools

Thomas K. Capozzoli, Ed.d.

and

R. Steve McVey, M.P.A.

S^t_L

St. Lucie Press
Boca Raton London
New York Washington, D.C.

Library of Congress Cataloging-in-Publication Data

Capozzoli, Thomas.
   Kids killing kids : managing violence and gangs in schools / Thomas K. Capozzoli, R.
Steve McVey.
       p.   cm.
   Includes bibliographical references and index.
   ISBN 1-57444-283-X (alk. paper)
     1.School violence—United States—Prevention. 2. Schools—United States—Safety
   measures.
  I. McVey, R. Steve. II. Title.
    LB3013.3 .C37   1999
    371.7′82′0973—dc21   99-052301
                                                  CIP

© 2000 by CRC Press LLC
Lewis Publishers is an imprint of CRC Press LLC

No claim to original U.S. Government works
International Standard Book Number 1-57444-283-X
Library of Congress Card Number 99-052301
Printed in the United States of America   3 4 5 6 7 8 9 0
Printed on acid-free paper

Introduction

As university professors, we are steeped in the tradition of scientific research as the only legitimate source of truth. However, before coming to academe, each of us lived and worked in the so-called "real world" for over 30 years where we learned to be astute observers of human nature. Each of us brings forth a balance of theory and scientific method from academe and the actuality and practicality of empiricism. We are fully aware that scientific purists may discard many of our observations and assertions as "unsupported" by formal research. If, as social scientists might assert, the answers were to be found so methodically, then why, haven't these critical problems of school violence and gangs already been solved? We believe that the simple linearity of the scientific method is not totally sufficient to the task of explaining such a complex, dynamic, social phenomenon.

The research for this book began more than a year ago. It was a natural progression of our book on workplace violence since many of the situations that have taken place in schools mirror workplace violence although the causes may be somewhat different. The book was almost finished when, while the nation watched on television, a tragedy unfolded in Littleton, CO. There was still some work to do on the book when a school shooting happened in Conyers, GA. After these tragedies, people looked for someone to blame and there were and still are numerous overreactions. Ann Beeson of the ACLU was quoted in *Time* magazine on May 10, 1999, that "There is a danger that schools are interpreting being different as being dangerous. Any nonconformist kid fits some sort of profile of a killer." We would go so far as to say that there are any number of kids, nonconformists or not, who could fit someone's profile of a killer. There have been calls for more gun control and less violence on television, in the movies and video games. On May 10, 1999, the president had a conference with media people from Hollywood on what to do about violence in the media. But no matter how many reactions or overreactions to this tragedy, there is no substitute for being proactive.

This book is both descriptive in that it describes many of the violent situations that have happened in the past several years in schools and prescriptive as to what schools can do to be proactive in trying to and prevent further situations. If we knew how to prevent violence in society, we would have done so long ago but we don't and all violent situations are not preventable but many of them may not have to be so tragic.

How do we find out who are potentially violent students? Once we do find out, what do we do with them? Are there some students who go over the "edge" because of the intolerable situations they endure in schools everyday, situations that find them outcast among other students, tormented and teased so unbearably they can no longer stand the torture? Do we have an epidemic of children who have psychological problems that go undetected until they come out in a tragic situation? What role do the parents play in school violence? Are the parents really responsible for children who carry out school violence? We're sure that these are not all of the questions that are asked or even need to be asked. But there are some methods that educators and parents can use to maybe reduce or prevent these situations from happening.

Gangs are also a problem in many schools because gangs are a source of school violence and many other problems. Gangs have been in inner-city schools for many years and now gangs are recruiting new members in some suburban schools. Gang violence has increased and many of the violent situations that happen in schools are the result of conflicts between rival gangs. Even the Trench Coat Mafia could be considered a gang. The history of gangs and what schools can do to keep gangs from starting, or growing in the school population, may inhibit future problems with gang violence.

The Authors

Dr. Thomas K. Capozzoli is an associate professor of organizational leadership at Purdue University. He is also a senior consultant with Personnel Services Inc., Carmel, IN, and a research associate of the National Center for the Management of Workplace Violence. Dr. Capozzoli spent 30 years with General Motors Corp., retiring in 1992. During his time with GM, he was involved in management, labor relations, and internal consulting. He received a doctorate in education in 1987 from Ball State University. He is the coauthor of *Managing Violence in the Workplace.*

R. Steve McVey is President and CEO of Personnel Services, Inc., Carmel, IN, a management, human resources, and organizational development consulting firm. He also is an associate professor of organizational leadership at Purdue University and a research associate in the National Center for the Management of Workplace Violence. Prior to his teaching appointment, Professor McVey served for 26 years as a Special Agent of the Federal Bureau of Investigation, during which he was involved in the psychological analysis of a variety of violent criminal behaviors. He holds a Master of Public Administration degree from Baruch College of the City University of New York.

Dedication

To my wonderful wife Susan and my children Tony, Casey, and Nick who always support me in whatever I do and you are the reason I do it.

Special Dedication

To the memory of a unique and wonderful person, Jackie McVey, who loved children and would be very happy to know this book has been completed.

Acknowledgement

We wish to thank Lieutenant Thomas A. DiNardo, Director of Crime Prevention/Community Relations of the Kokomo Police Department, Kokomo, Indiana for the information and data he provided about gangs in the United States.

Table of Contents

1 Cases of Violence in Schools

On Tuesday, April 20, 1999, the country was shocked to hear that two 18-year-old boys, Eric Harris and Dylan Klebold, at Columbine High School in Littleton, CO, committed one of the largest mass-slaying of students in school in our country's history. Columbine is a school of about 1,900 students. The boys started their rampage at about 11: 15 A.M. when they entered Columbine High, started shooting and spreading bombs. When the shooting and bombing were over, there were 15 dead, 12 students, one teacher, and the two shooters, plus many injured. The two shooters, Harris and Klebold, had taken their own lives.

Investigations since the tragedy have detailed some startling facts about the two boys. It seems as if this situation might have been averted if students, teachers, and parents had understood the signs that Harris and Klebold had exhibited. If someone had only let authorities or school officials know what they had said they were planning, what might have been the outcome? Unfortunately, it was found that people did know—people had reported the fact that at least one of the boys had exhibited symptoms, that there was some sort of problem, but the reports went unheeded. If these reports had been followed up, Columbine may never have happened.

Since it did happen, the first question people have asked is why did these two boys from middle-class homes perpetrate this atrocity? From reports in the news, they belonged to a gang called the "Trench Coat Mafia." They espoused hate messages and felt picked on by other students, mainly athletes. Also, according to a diary kept by one of the boys, they had been planning this rampage for a year. They had detailed everything, from where they would hide to the hand signals they would use while killing. One boy had an internet website that espoused hate messages and told of the date the tragedy would happen. They had pipe bombs they planted in cars and in the school, and there was a propane bomb planted in the school kitchen; had it gone off the tragedy would have been much greater. There were enough bombs planted that they must have had access to the school during the evening or night hours. Most of the bombs could not have been carried in during the shooting spree.

The two were supposedly avid followers of Adolf Hitler. They reportedly wore swastikas on black shirts, spoke German in the halls, used the Nazi salute, and even planned the shooting for Hitler's birthday. They reportedly learned enough of the German language to berate their classmates. They also played the most vicious video games and talked about who they hated and would like to kill. At one point, one of the boys' English teachers brought him to the attention of a guidance counselor because the work he was doing was so violent. The boys also made a tape for a video production class in which they were pretending to shoot all of the athletes with a rifle.

Both boys had been in trouble with authorities on one occasion. In January 1998, they were arrested for breaking into a commercial van and stealing electronic equipment. They were convicted of the felony and entered the juvenile court rehabilitation program that was designed to help them clear their records by participating in community service programs and anger management seminars. Both finished the program early because they were touted as model participants. Unfortunately, because the two committed suicide, many of the questions as to specifically why they committed this mass slaying will forever go unanswered. There will be much speculation and authorities have pieced together much of what went on but there will still be speculation.

An incident like this raises an important question: Are our schools safe? Some experts say statistics indicate that schools are safe and although there are incidents of violence they are not of the magnitude that some might think. However, when you look at the Columbine High massacre and some of the other incidents of school violence, how much do statistics really mean if it happens in your school?

What type of child commits these atrocious crimes? Why do they happen? What can be done about them? Are they predictable? What happens when these crimes are committed? Are they preventable? These are not simple questions to answer and all of them might not be answerable in the ways that people would like to hear. In this book, we hope to provide answers to these questions and detail ways that schools, like any other organization, can deal with the potential child who would perpetuate such crimes. After all, when parents send their children to school, they expect them to return home. A school should be a safe place for children.

Since the Littleton massacre, there have been some near misses. In Wimberly, TX, a small town of about 3,000 southwest of Austin, four 14-year-old eighth-grade boys were taken into custody on April 23, 1999, just three days after Littleton, for conspiracy to commit murder, arson, and the manufacture of explosives. It seems they had begun planning the attack on their junior high school in January. Because of Littleton, someone had reported what the boys were planning and it was stopped before it happened.

On April 22, 1999, in Jackson, WY, a 17-year-old student was arrested when authorities found a metal device and a fuse in his backpack. And, on April 23, 1999, in Princess Anne, MD, a high school senior was arrested when he threatened to "blow up" the school. In Bakersfield, CA, a 13-year-old was taken out of school because his classmates spotted him loading a .40-caliber handgun. Five teens were arrested at William McKinley Junior High School in Brooklyn, NY, after they had boasted about plans to blow up the school on graduation day. Since Littleton, there have also been many other instances of suspensions of teenagers wearing black trench coats and making threats.

Exactly one month after the shooting in Littleton, T. J. Solomon, a sophomore at Heritage High School in Conyers, GA, opened fire on students with a .22-caliber rifle. Heritage is a school of about 1,300 students. Heritage High fortunately was not another Littleton but it was nevertheless a school shooting with a number of students being injured, none life-threatening. However, the pattern of this shooting was similar to other school shootings; a student with a weapon was intent on injuring other students. Solomon entered the school with the rifle and a handgun at about 7: 55 A.M. and started shooting. Many students thought it was a joke but when blood was spotted, it became apparent that it was not. The shooting spree did not last long and Solomon was talked into surrendering by the school's assistant principal.

In an interview on national television, one student said, "I didn't think it would happen here." Heritage High School is a "good" school in an affluent suburb of Atlanta. Solomon lives in a $275,000 home in a subdivision. His stepfather is an executive and his mother is a secretary. Again, the question is, why the shooting? Solomon had recently broken up with his girlfriend and was distraught over the fact that this relationship had ended. He had also been treated for depression in the past year, his grades had been falling, and he was being treated with a drug for hyperactivity. In the past, he had threatened to bomb a classroom and had told a friend that he was considering suicide. No one reported either of these threats and some speculated that the shooting was even a cry for help because Solomon did not shoot at students in a manner that would indicate his intent to kill them. Most of the shots were aimed low. Solomon is held in a juvenile detention center and there is a possibility he will be tried as an adult.

Other Instances of School Violence

Bath, MI

The most deadly massacre of school children came on May 18, 1927, when a so-called "demented" farmer planted dynamite in the Bath Consolidated School and detonated it from his car. Thirty-eight school children were killed along with several adults and many children were injured. The farmer's wife worked for the school and he killed her before making the assault on the school. Officials determined he had planned this for some time as it took time for him to wire the explosives in the school. Several other dynamite bombs did not go off and had they, many more lives would have been lost.

Springfield, OR

Springfield, OR is a working-class town of about 51,000 people about 110 miles south of Portland. Thurston High School, located in Springfield, is a school of about 1,350 students. On May 21, 1998, shots rang out in the cafeteria leaving two students dead, four students critically injured, six seriously injured and eleven other students injured. In all, 19 students were hit by the gunfire. All of the shooting was done by a student, Kipland P. Kinkel. As Kinkel fired on the students with a semi-automatic weapon, he displayed an eerie calmness that one would not expect from a high school freshman. Witnesses said students ran for cover and dived under tables to avoid the bullets. One student commented, "It was just sort of happening in slow motion." At the beginning, some students thought it was not real but it soon became a frightening reality. When Kinkel walked into the cafeteria, he was wearing a trench coat and was armed with .22-caliber rifle, a .22-caliber handgun, and a Glock handgun. Kinkel was finally subdued by other students as he was preparing to reload and fire more rounds.

Kinkel had been suspended from Thurston the day before the shooting. In fact, he was expelled for bringing a gun to school, after the school had gotten a tip. He was arrested and charged with the possession of a stolen firearm, then released to his parents' custody. His parents were found murdered in their home. The school superintendent said that they were considering whether Kinkel should be expelled from school for the possession of the gun.

Kip Kinkel had been in trouble with the police before, for throwing rocks at cars from an overpass. According to a fellow student, "He always said it would be fun to kill someone and do stuff like that." In fact, Kinkel had told other people that he was probably going to do something stupid to get back at the people who had suspended him from school. Some students also said that Kinkel had once given a speech in class on how to make a bomb because he was fascinated with explosives. Students knew that he had a dark side, a "hair-trigger" temper and at one time had bragged about torturing animals. He allegedly listened to the music of Marilyn Manson. According to other reports, Kinkel's parents knew of his problems and they were making efforts to help him. Kinkel will be tried as an adult in Oregon.

Edinboro, PA

About 100 miles north of Pittsburgh lies the rural town of Edinboro. It is a peaceful area. At least it was peaceful until Friday night April 24, 1998, when an eighth-grade student, 14-year-old Andrew Wurst from James Parker Middle School, burst into a school dance and opened fire, killing a teacher and wounding two other students and another teacher.

Wurst, whose nickname was "Satan," had discussed plans to kill people he hated. According to friends of Wurst, the teenager liked to smoke marijuana and listen to the ghoulish sounds of the musical group called Marilyn Manson. As early as a month before the shooting, Wurst had told friends that he was going to use his father's gun to kill people he hated and then kill himself. Other students, who knew Wurst, said that the teenager talked about how he would make the dance a "memorable" evening. However, everyone thought it was a joke and that he was just a shy, quirky student with an offbeat sense of humor who had a dislike for school and frustrated anger toward his parents. Wurst was also described as a loner who never smiled and would often dress sloppily, with untucked T-shirts and untied shoes. Wurst is to be tried as an adult.

Jonesboro, AR

Jonesboro is a town of about 46,000 people in the northeast corner of Arkansas. On Thursday, March 24, 1998 at the West-side Middle School, Jonesboro became infamous for violence committed by the youngest mass murderers in this country's history. West-side is a school of about 250 students. Two boys, Andrew Golden, 11, and Mitchell Johnson, 13, gunned down 15 students as they exited the middle school building after Golden had pulled the fire alarm. Four students and one teacher were killed and the others wounded.

According to the reports, Golden, who owned a personal arsenal of guns, had learned to shoot a gun almost as soon as he had learned to walk, and he was described as a gun enthusiast. He was also described by one neighbor as "often seen running around the neighborhood in camouflage gear and he seemed evil-acting. He was always threatening people." Some neighbors described Golden as the type of kid they didn't want their children playing with. Another neighbor said, "Golden was a sweet child when his parents were around but when he was away from his parents he was a demon." He allegedly had a "filthy mouth." According to *Time* magazine, Johnson's mother alleges that it was Golden's idea for the shooting. Golden's parents were very safety conscious and kept the guns locked so they were not accessible to the boy. The boys finally had to steal the weapons used in the ambush from Golden's grandfather.

Mitchell Johnson was not a native of Jonesboro, having moved there from Minnesota about two years before the episode. There are different reports as to the type of personality traits that Johnson exhibited. Some described him as a church-going young man who was very polite. Just a few days before the shooting, Johnson's family said he had gone to a nursing home to sing with a church group. A pastor at Johnson's church described his conduct as "well-mannered and polite and that he was one who never had to be called down."

Some people described him as a "bully" who liked to pick on kids, brandished a knife in school, and wanted to be a gang member. He had also told classmates that "he had a lot of killing to do." Johnson's girlfriend had recently broken up with him and he allegedly took her rebuff very hard. According to one of Johnson's classmates, he had said he was going to shoot his ex-girlfriend and then kill everyone else in the building. His ex-girlfriend was wounded in the shooting. Another classmate said that Johnson always wore red every day as a sign he was a member of the "Bloods" gang. She also said that he spoke about wanting "to hurt people" and on the Monday prior to the shootings he had told her, "Tomorrow you all will find out if you live or die."

Johnson and Golden, because of the law in the State of Arkansas, cannot be tried as adults. They will be treated as juveniles and they could be out of custody as early as 18 years of age. Johnson did plead guilty and Golden was found guilty but their records are sealed because they are juveniles and essentially they will have no record.

West Paducah, KY

West Paducah is located in far-western Kentucky 10 miles west of Paducah. Heath High School is a part of the McCracken County school district that includes three high schools, three middle schools, and six elementary schools. Heath is the smallest of the high schools, with an enrollment of about 600 students. On Monday morning, December 1, 1997, West Paducah and Heath became the center of a tragic shooting.

Michael Carneal, age 14, a freshman at Heath High School, had talked to more than one other student about a possible shooting at the school. Carneal, according to reports, was something of a misfit at Heath. He wore ill-fitting, loud-colored clothes and on occasion had disciplinary problems. The principal of the school indicated that he thought Carneal had some maturity problems but also said there had been no indications of violence in his background and he was not considered dangerous.

On the morning of December 1, Carneal killed three classmates and injured five others with guns he had stolen. The victims had been involved in a school prayer meeting with several other students. Just as the meeting broke up, Carneal fired his first shots. Carneal had warned a fellow student not to attend the prayer group meeting on that morning but did not indicate to the student why he should not attend. The student did not report the incident to any school officials or any other adults. Carneal allegedly had gotten the idea for the killings from the violence in the movie *The Basketball Diaries.* Carneal has never offered an explanation for the shooting and he will be tried as an adult.

Pearl, MS

Pearl is a blue-collar suburb of Mississippi's state capital of Jackson with a population of about 22,000. On the morning of October 1, 1997, Pearl became infamous. On that morning, Luke Woodham, 16-year-old sophomore at Pearl High School, entered the school with a .30–30 hunting rifle and opened fire on students. Pearl High School has about 1,000 students. In the 11-minute rampage, Woodham killed two students and wounded seven others. Woodham had come to school that morning wearing a baggy overcoat to conceal the rifle. He went to the school commons area, walked up behind a fellow sophomore, killed her and then began to methodically move through the area firing at his other victims. The school principal said he was "cool and calm" as the committed the massacre.

As quickly as the carnage began, it ended as Woodham left the school. According to reports, he got into his car and tried to flee but lost control and came to a stop. The principal, who had retrieved a gun from his truck, got to Woodham and held him until police arrived. When the principal asked him why he had done this, Woodham's comment to him was, "The world has wronged me." It was later learned that schoolmates were not his only victims. Police found Woodham's mother at home where he had killed her with a knife before going to school.

According to reports, Woodham had erratic coping skills, was very sensitive to being teased, did not like insults, and lacked empathy for others. His father had left the family when Woodham was 11 years old and Woodham's girlfriend had recently broken up with him.

In a strange twist to the Pearl story, it was later learned that there was a larger plot that included several other boys from Pearl. According to the reports, these boys had planned from the beginning of the school year to attack the school. They would often meet at Woodham's home to discuss their plans. It seems that only Woodham was serious enough to carry out the plot. Woodham was sentenced to three life sentences in the Mississippi State Penitentiary.

Bethel, AK

Bethel, AK is a small community of about 4,600 in the southwestern part of the state. Bethel lost its innocence on February 19, 1997, when 16-year-old Evan Ramsey, a Bethel Regional High School student, killed the principal and a member of the basketball team and wounded three other students. One schoolgirl who knew the accused killer said he had alerted friends to his plans days earlier but no one let anyone know about the plans.

Bethel is a very isolated community in Alaska. With the isolation there was a sense of safety. Although Bethel had its share of domestic violence, no one thought something like this would happen there in the middle of the Alaska wilderness. Ramsey was convicted as an adult and sentenced to two 99-year prison terms.

Moses Lake, WA

Moses Lake is 179 miles east of Seattle in the heart of the Columbia River basin, a desolate area. However, with the building of the Grand Coulee Dam came irrigation and farming. A sign outside of town says, "Welcome to Moses Lake, the Desert Oasis." On a cold February 2, 1996, 14-year-old Barr Loukaitis, an honor student at Frontier Junior High School, held his 10th grade algebra class hostage with a hunting rifle, eventually killing his 49-year-old teacher and two 15-year-old students. Loukaitis took the guns from his father. According to reports, Loukaitis had several personal problems. According to Loukaitis' mother, he had been a friendly and outgoing child but began withdrawing from people when the family started to have problems and her marriage began to fall apart. Loukaitis became obsessed with guns, death, and killing. He had several books by author Stephen King and one of King's books in particular, *Rage* about a teenager who kills his teacher and holds his algebra class hostage was found on Loukaitis' nightstand. Police also found a Clint Eastwood video in a videocassette recorder cued to the part where Eastwood's character is standing over a victim holding a rifle.

Family problems were not the only problems Loukaitis had. He was teased relentlessly by the bigger boys at school about his slight build. One of the boys who teased him was Manuel Vela, Jr. Loukaitis talked of wanting to kill Vela and asked some of his friends what they would think if he killed him. These friends did not take him seriously. He also told friends that it would be "cool" to kill people or to go across country killing people like in the movie *Natural Born Killers*. Julia Moore, a psychologist who treated Loukaitis after the shootings, said "he saw so much evil in the world that he began seeing himself as some sort of avenger."

On the day of the attack, Loukaitis burst into the algebra class about 10 minutes after the class had started and took steps toward Manuel Vela, whom he had threatened to kill. He fired three shots, hitting three students. Vela, being the closest, died instantly. The teacher moved toward Loukaitis but crouched and turned when he pointed the gun at her and killed her with one shot. Classmates said that he turned to them and said, "This sure beats algebra class, doesn't it?" This was a line from Stephen King's book, *Rage*.

During the trial, in which he was tried as an adult, the prosecutor portrayed Loukaitis as a very "angry young man" who was angry at the girls who were rude to him. His attorney portrayed Loukaitis as a victim of bipolar personality disorder. However, Loukaitis was tried and convicted as an adult and sentenced to two life terms and 205 years in prison.

Tavares, FL

Tavares, FL is located in Lake County, about 25 miles northwest of the Magic Kingdom in Orlando. It is a community of farmers and retirees, and most thought it was a place where school violence would happen. On Friday, September 29, 1995, the local middle school became the scene of a shooting. Fourteen-year-old Keith Johnson shot and fatally wounded a 13-year-old classmate. It was unclear why the shooting occurred but some classmates thought that the victim did not like gangs and the shooter was a gang member. Others thought that the victim was the person who always bullied Johnson and he had decided not to take it any longer.

People interviewed in Tavares were shocked that the shooting had happened. A comment from one native of Tavares said, "I've heard of incidents like this in other places, but I thought we were immune [to it] here." Johnson was tried as an adult.

Carter County, KY

On January 18, 1993, Scott Pennington, 17, of Rush, KY shot and killed a teacher and a janitor at East Carter High School. He then held 22 classmates hostage at gunpoint for about 15 minutes before finally surrendering. Pennington was described as a quiet and bright student who had few friends but was passive. People who described him said that even when ridiculed or hit by other students, he remained passive. Pennington was convicted as an adult and sentenced to life without parole.

Other Cases of School Violence and Near-School Violence

Clay Shrout, 17, of Union, KY, shot his parents and two sisters before going to Larry A. Ryle High School in Union, on May 26, 1994. Shrout was five minutes late when he walked into his trigonometry class with his prom date in tow. He showed no emotion as he pulled a pistol from his waist and announced he was holding the class hostage. When a student ask him why, he replied, "I have had a really bad day, I've just killed my family." Shrout held the class hostage for about 30 minutes before giving up to police. Shrout was found guilty but mentally ill and sentenced to life in prison and no parole for 25 years.

On November 15, 1995, Jamie Rouse, a 17-year-old high school senior from Lynnville, TN, killed a teacher and a student and wounded another teacher. He was using a stolen rifle. He was having mounting academic difficulties. Rouse was convicted as an adult and sentenced to life in prison without parole.

On September 15, 1995, at George Rogers Clark High School in Clark County, KY, Daniel Watson held a fellow student at gunpoint. He had been in a fight before school, went home, and returned with two guns, taking the student hostage.

On January 23, 1995, John Sirola, 14, an eighth-grader at Sacred Heart High School in California, wounded the high school principal. He shot the principal in the face with a sawed-off shotgun. The trigger for the shooting was the school's insistence he wear a uniform. Sirola was killed when he accidentally shot himself while fleeing the scene.

On September 18, 1989, at Jackson County High School near McKee, KY, Dustin Pierce, 17, took 11 classmates hostage. Pierce, who was described as quiet and bright, walked into his second period history class and fired at least two shotgun blasts and then took his classmates hostage. He was demanding to see his father whom he had not seen in 13 years. He surrendered peacefully.

In Norwalk, CA on October 24, 1997, Khoa Truc "Robert" Dang, 21, a former student at John Glenn High School returned to campus to kill his ex-girlfriend and then kill himself in front of dozens of students who stood horrified. Dang graduated from the school in 1994 and was an honors graduate.

Indianapolis, IN is known as the crossroads of the U.S. On April 16, 1998, a 17-year-old alternative education student was arrested after he was observed by a security officer, placing bullets into a pistol in the parking lot. Alternative education in Indianapolis is a program for expelled students. The student caught for possession of the gun had already been expelled from a traditional high school for possession of marijuana.

This arrest came after two eight-year-old students in elementary schools were arrested for possession of guns in the school. One of the eight-year-olds had pointed a loaded gun at another student but the gun jammed and would not fire. To curb the problem of elementary children bringing guns to school, a program of randomly searching elementary school children was started. Seven years ago, the city school system started searching high school and middle school children but now the practice has been expanded because of problems in the elementary schools.

In Memphis, TN, a five-year-old kindergarten pupil was arrested after he brought a loaded .25-caliber semiautomatic pistol to school to kill his teacher for punishing him with a "timeout" period. Timeout is a form of discipline for young children. The child allegedly had said he wanted to kill several students as well as the teacher who had disciplined him.

In Gas City, IN, five students were suspended from school and others were under investigation when a teacher found a letter that contained cult references and a threat to kill one of the school's 638 students on the last day of school.

In Fayetteville, TN, a high school senior shot and killed another senior three days before they were to graduate. The two had apparently been arguing over a girlfriend.

In St. Charles, MO, three sixth-grade students were arrested after classmates told school officials that the boys were planning to shoot some of their classmates on the last day of school.

Violent Trends

School violence can be defined as any act of intimidation, threats, harassment, robbery, vandalism, physical assault such as fights, with or without a weapon (including rape, and other sexual battery), or murder that happens on school grounds or buses going to and from school. Many schools have what is termed a "zero tolerance" for school violence. In other words, violence in any of the identified forms will not be tolerated and if it happens, the perpetrator of the violence will be not be allowed to attend school (or some other predetermined consequence). This expulsion may be permanent or for an extended period of time (this may also include filing criminal charges against the student, depending on the violation).

In a report from the National Center for Education Statistics (NCES) for the school year for 1996–97, approximately 57% of public elementary and secondary schools reported one or more incidents of violence or a crime that was reported to law enforcement officials (many incidents of violence may not be reported to law enforcement officials because the school officials will try to handle it themselves). Ten percent of public schools reported one or more *serious* violent crimes that were reported to law enforcement officials. There were approximately 190,000 incidents of physical attacks or fights without a weapon and about 11,000 incidents of physical attacks or fights where a weapon was used. The U.S. Department of Justice also estimates that every day in the U.S., 100,000+ children carry some type of weapon to school and these are mainly guns and as many as 40 children are injured or killed by guns. Teachers, students, and law enforcement believe that the reason these children carry weapons is:

- For protection in school from aggressors
- For impressing their friends
- To increase their self esteem
- For protection going to and from school

According to the NCES report, elementary schools reported fewer serious violent crimes such as physical attacks (with or without a weapon). Public high schools were more likely than elementary schools to have serious violence problems. Also, according to the U.S. Centers for Disease Control the rate of urban students being killed on or near campus is nine times higher than in small towns or rural communities. Victims and perpetrators of school violence represent all racial, ethnic, and economic groups. Males are more likely to be involved in acts of violence although females are becoming more and more involved in these acts.

One of the interesting facts about school violence in the 1998–1999 school year is that school-related deaths dropped from a peak in 1992–1993 to a low of 24 in 1998–1999 and if it had not been for the Columbine mass murders, the number of deaths would have been at an all-time low for this decade at nine.

Victims of School Violence

The victims of school violence cover a broad spectrum. Students in all grades are subject to violence, and students are not the only victims of violence. Although teachers believe they are not likely to be victims of violence, they are also at risk for a violent act. There were teachers killed in Littleton, CO; Edinboro, PA; Jonesboro, AR; Bethel, AK; Moses Lake, WA; and Carter County, KY. Some of these teachers really had no relationship to the perpetrator of the violence but they were still killed. In most instances, the perpetrator of the violence kills at random without the thought of killing specific students or teacher.

School Violence Statistics

According to the CDC:

- 83% of school homicide or suicide victims were male
- 28% of shootings happened in the school
- 36% happened outdoors on school property
- 35% happened off-campus
- 65% of school-associated violent deaths were students
- 11% were teachers or other staff members
- 23% were community members who were killed on school property
- The total number of violent events has decreased steadily since 1992 but the total number of multiple-victim events has increased

According to the Center for the Study and Prevention of Violence at the University of Colorado, "Many school-aged children can easily obtain firearms even though the law forbids the sale of firearms to a minors."

Youth Violence Statistics

Many experts identify kids as ticking bombs in society and others see youth violence as merely "overblown" by the media. Some experts cite the easy access to weapons such as guns as the reason youth violence has increased in the last few years. They have indicated that all around the country, young people are taking up guns as a method of solving their conflicts. According to statistics from the Justice Department compiled by James Alan Fox, professor of criminal justice at

Northeastern University, and Marianne W. Zawitz, Justice Department statistician:

- Homicide victim rates for 14- to 17-year-olds increased almost 150% from 1985 to 1993.
- Since 1993, homicide rates for teens and young adults have declined but are still considerably higher than the levels of the 1980s.
- Homicides committed by younger offenders are more likely to involve multiple offenders.
- The number of homicides involving adult or juvenile gang violence has increased by sevenfold since 1976.
- Teenagers and young adults were more likely to become victims of violent crime than older persons.
- In 1996, students age 12 to 18 were victims of about 225,000 incidents of nonfatal serious violent crime at school.
- In 1996–1997:
  - 10% of all public schools reported at least one serious violent crime.
  - 47% reported at least one less serious or nonviolent crime.
  - 43% of public schools did not report any of these crimes to the police.
- The percent of 12th graders injured in violence at school has not changed over the 20-year-period from 1976 to 1996 although, the percentage of those threatened with injury showed a very slight upward trend.
- From 1992–1996, teachers were victims of about 316,000 nonfatal and property crimes at school including 18,000 serious violent crimes.
- There was no change in the percent of students reporting any violent or property victimization (14.5% versus 14.6% violent) between 1989–1995.
- The percent of students reporting street gang presence at school nearly doubled between 1989 and 1995 from 15.3% to 28.4%.

From the data presented by the CDC and the Justice Department, there must be some concern for the increase in youth violent crime but it does not mean that all young people are bad.

2 The Aftereffects of School Violence

I t is difficult to measure the aftereffects or the costs of school violence. In the workplace, the Occupational Safety and Health Act (OSHA) says that a safe workplace must be provided. When a violent act occurs, current estimates of the cost to the workplace is around $2 million per episode. It is also easier to measure lost productivity or sales in the workplace. In the school, we don't have sales and not too many people are interested in the productivity of students or teachers. However, there are costs and postviolence effects that we may not realize.

Psychological — Students who witness or are directly involved in a violent act can and often do suffer psychological damage. This psychological trauma may persist throughout the lives of the individuals and may cost them in relationships with others, in their ability to be effective employees, or by never allowing them to feel completely safe again. These may be costs that are not readily visible but nevertheless are quite real to the individuals.

Families of victims — The families of victims of school violence will live with the tragedy the rest of their lives. Families of students who were killed will always wonder what that person would or could have been. Losing a child, especially to unnecessary violence, is difficult for them or anyone else to understand. Families whose children have been injured may have to care for the children for the rest of their lives because of the seriousness of the injuries.

Families of the killer(s) — The families of the killers will also have to live with what their children have done. They may blame themselves for what has happened or they may not understand why their child became a killer. From other members of the community, they may be blamed for the shooting as if they actually committed the crime themselves. In some instances, the immediate families of the killers were the first victims, leaving other relatives to speculate what went wrong in the family to cause this to happen. In some situations, family members may be forced to move from their homes and leave the city in which they live in because of speculation about the family and how it spawned a killer.

Property damage — Facilities and equipment are damaged and must be replaced and private property of victims can be damaged. These costs will vary from school to school but they may be quite high in some situations. In Littleton, there was substantial damage to the building from the bullets, the bombs, and the water that came from the sprinkler system. In some instances, students will not want to return to a school where there has been a shooting causing enrollment to drop in that school.

Legal fees — Taxpayers, and in many cases, families will incur the costs to prosecute and defend the perpetrators of school violence. If convicted, taxpayers also shoulder the cost to incarcerate them. Once convicted, the shooters may be given life terms, and this will cost the taxpayers to house them as long as they live. That cost will escalate every year.

There will also be the cost of lawsuits filed by the families of the victims. In Littleton, there has been a $250 million lawsuit filed by the parents of one of the victims who was killed in the shooting. According to the attorney for the parents, who appeared on *The Today Show* on NBC on May 27, 1999, the suit will be against the parents of the two killers and anyone who might have had responsibility for the situation. Each person named in the lawsuit will have to retain legal counsel and this will be at their expense. These expenses may run into the thousands of dollars.

Preventive measures — Schools must now implement new procedures and/or additional security personnel/equipment that may be needed in order to inhibit or prevent similar occurrences in the future. Most schools were not built with the thought of security in mind and to update them for more protection will require the school systems to spend considerable amounts of money.

There is probably no concrete way to measure all of the aftereffects of school violence. Every time a school violence incident happens we will learn more about the aftereffects. However, the one thing we have unfortunately learned in studying workplace and school violence is that there will be more incidents.

3 Causes of School Violence

School violence of the magnitude of recent years is a new phenomenon and has not occurred in sufficient numbers to enable definitive conclusions to be made about the causes, predictions, or solutions. However, in the mass killings that have occurred or the potential for mass killings, this question always comes up: What type of young person commits or would commit such an act? Once a profile has been developed for the perpetrator, the next child to commit this act may not fit it. There is always the potential that every classroom or school in this country could be harboring a potential mass killer. It is not specifically known how many children and adolescents in the U.S. may have serious psychological problems. According to estimates, as many as one of every four children has some form of disorder and one out of every five has a moderate or severe disorder. Even if it was known that a juvenile has a serious psychological problem, no one knows specifically what the trigger event might be to cause a particular juvenile to become a killer.

One of the best predictors of future behavior is past behavior. If a child has a past of violence or some type of erratic behavior, the chances are greater that this child will demonstrate this same type of behavior sometime in the future. The only problem is, when in the future will this happen? In our book, *Managing Violence in the Workplace,* there are some specific definite actions by managers, fellow workers, etc., that might cause a person to become violent. Some of these similar conditions, which can trigger violence, can and do exist in schools. One of the consistent themes that runs through most of the school killings is the fact that most of the killers were children who at one time or another had been ridiculed or teased by classmates. Many of the killers were seen as "different" by their classmates. However, many children are seen as different by classmates or at times feel they are being ridiculed but they never resort to violence to deal with these situations.

Many of the schools in which violent acts of mass murder have been committed are considered to be "good" schools. Most people are not surprised when acts of violence occur in what is considered to be an inner city school. People believe that these schools have drug and gang problems which makes them more prone to violent actions by students. But mass murders are not happening in inner city schools; they are happening in suburban schools that are in or near what are considered to be affluent neighborhoods. These aren't the type of schools that one would suspect to be harboring the next mass killers. On *The Today Show,* one superintendent of a school that had suffered a shooting said that she had been in the school in recent weeks and everything seemed to be normal. Obviously, one must consider the fact that if everything looks normal, it still may not be normal.

Categories of School Violence

There are three categories of perpetrators of school violence: students, former students, and nonstudents. There are also three types of situations, based upon the origin of the conflict and the location where it occurs:

Type 1: Violence originates at school and occurs in the school. A situation at school develops, often as a result of a chain of events, to cause a student to feel that he or she is a victim of unfair treatment. The student then seeks to exact vengeance upon, or obtain retribution from the antagonist(s) and/or to make an example of them. The antagonists may be identified from among teachers, fellow students, school workers, relatives, or others. Other victims may be people who just happen to be there when the incident occurs and the killers may really have no grudge against them. In many cases, the victims are not specifically chosen by the perpetrator (as in most of the school violence situations, many innocent bystanders are killed) but they are killed or injured to satisfy the retribution or vengeance needs of the perpetrator.

Type 2: Violence originates in the school but occurs outside the school. A situation develops in the school but the perpetrator does not choose to exact retribution or vengeance inside the school building. In this case the perpetrator will choose some other location to "get" the victim. All situations do not end in murder but can lead to destruction of the property or in a fight between two or more individuals, with or without a weapon.

Type 3: Violence originates outside the school and occurs in the school. This was the situation in Norwalk, CA where the student returned to his former school to kill his exgirlfriend. Another situation that can occur is a bomb threat to the school. This happens quite frequently to many schools and can be the work of a disgruntled student or someone wanting vengeance on the school system.

There are a variety of complex causes of violence in the schools and more than one cause can be attributed to a single incident. When violence happens in school there are always experts who have explanations depending on their perspective. If there was just one reason, the problem of school violence might be easily solved.

In the case of children, when situations do arise that could cause violence they may not have the emotional coping skills to understand the situation, or the necessary interpersonal skills (such as conflict management skills) to deal with the situation.

Personality Conflicts

Interpersonal conflicts among students, and students and teachers, are probably the most frequent and apparent causes of school violence. "Apparent" is emphasized because often there are other significant personal factors that children have brought with them to school, and the conflicts are a result of those underlying problems. In such an event, the conflicts at school may be more difficult to resolve. The school situation, many times, is a convenient means of displacing or projecting these underlying frustrations. The conflict at school then simply becomes the straw that breaks the camel's back.

There are instances of legitimate personality conflicts with other students and teachers. Students are no different from adults in the fact that there are some people who rub others the wrong way. If the student does not have the necessary coping skills, the situation can develop into a negative cause-and-effect spiral that can ultimately become violent.

Personality is one's unique set of behavioral traits, including manners of expression and interaction with others. As one's personality develops through early childhood and into adolescence, it becomes more and more patterned and predictable. Personality is both complex and complicated. It embodies one's self-concept and self esteem (the degree to which a person believes that he or she is worthwhile and deserving). Although there are some normal personalities that are more interpersonally functional than others, there are others who are abnormal or disordered, even in children.

Although personality is affected by both heredity and environment, personality disorders are, by definition, learning disorders. The person has failed to learn appropriate and effective behavioral responses to some or several typical life frustrations. This may come from a dysfunctional family environment where inappropriate behavioral responses are observed by the child. It may also come from the school setting. Schools have an explicit mandate to socialize children into the norms and values of our cultures. Schools in this country foster competition through built-in systems of reward and punishment. A child who is working to learn a new skill important to the development of his or her personality can be made to feel stupid and unsuccessful.

Peer groups at school also have an important effect on the child's personality and how he or she is treated by a peer group can have an adverse on his or her personality. Peers can often be quite unfeeling when they make comments to other students that are negative or derogatory. This can cause a child to become a loner or gravitate toward other students who they perceive to be mistreated as they have been.

Some of these learning disorders result in a personality having an unrealistic perception of "rights" and "responsibilities," and the demand that his or her needs and preferences be satisfied before those others. These personalities are insensitive to the rights and privileges of others, and such people tend to be bossy, domineering, threatening, and even violent if they feel their own rights are threatened or they are wronged. As Luke Woodham commented in Pearl, MS, "The world has wronged me."

In many instances children have not developed sufficient control to govern their tempers nor do they possess the maturity to understand the total consequences of their violent acts. For example: When adults commit a violent act in the workplace, approximately 60% of them then take their own lives because they see this as the ultimate act and there is no reason to go on because they have exacted their revenge. In school shootings that have taken place, most students do not take their own lives after the event. This may indicate they do not really understand the consequences of their act or that they should not engage in the final act of killing themselves because there is still a future. In Littleton, the two students committed suicide in what might have been a suicide pact. The student in Edinboro, PA, stated that he was going to kill himself after he killed others but he did not do so. In Norwalk, CA, the former student killed himself but this case might also be considered "spillover" violence and the school was the best place for him to find his ex-girlfriend.

There are four basic personality dimensions:

1. Extroversion vs. introversion — This dimension ranges from the sociable, talkative, and assertive to the retiring, sober, reserved, and outwardly cautious.
2. Agreeableness — This spectrum ranges from the good-natured, gentle, and cooperative to the irritable and inflexible.

3. Conscientiousness — This ranges from careful, thorough, responsible, and self-disciplined to the irresponsible and unscrupulous.
4. Emotional stability — On one end, this type is calm, enthusiastic, and secure and on the other end, depressed, emotional, and insecure.

Personality also affects how one interprets the events that are occurring in one's life. Interpersonal relationships are a central part of a person's life. Relatives, peer group, and love interests normally have a significant influence on a person's perceptions, since they share the social values and interpretive biases of their common culture. If one willingly segregates oneself from normal personal bonds and social interactions or if one is not taught how to integrate into the culture, the person becomes divorced from the mainstream values and beliefs. The extent of the isolation from these cultures determines the degree to which the person thinks and acts on the basis of singularly personal logical constructs. Often, the resultant behaviors either are "out of step" with the mainstream cultures or simply inappropriate or ineffective.

Conduct Disorder

There seem to be some children who are indifferent to the rights of others. They will not yield to anyone else and they argue, threaten, cheat, and steal. They may demonstrate reckless behavior such as setting fires, jumping off roofs, or some type of cruel behaviors such as cruelty to animals. As these children grow older, they graduate to the violation of more major social norms and feel they are not bound by these social norms. They may commit assault, rape, or some other type of violent crime. These children are given the diagnosis of conduct disorder.

The *DSM-IV* criteria for this diagnosis fall into four categories:

1. Aggression against people or animals. Such children may be considered to be bullies and are often in fights. Kip Kinkel in Springfield, OR, had a history of cruelty to animals. Luke Woodham in Pearl, MS, had previously beaten his dog with a club and then set fire to it after wrapping it in a bag.
2. Destruction of property. They may set fires or vandalize property.
3. Deceitfulness or theft. They may shoplift or steal from others. Both Eric Harris and Dylan Klebold in Littleton, CO, had been convicted of theft.
4. Other violations of rules. They may be a truant or they may have run away from home.

If a person is under 18, has committed any three of these infractions in the last year (in any category), and shows poor adjustment at home or school, he or she qualifies for the diagnosis of conduct disorder.

Conduct disorder is one of the most common syndromes of childhood and adolescence. However, age of onset seems to be very important. The *DSM-IV* requires that the person diagnosing conduct disorder specify whether the child falls into the *childhood-onset type* (at least one symptom before the age of 10) or the *adolescent-onset type* (no symptoms prior to 10). When the onset of conduct disorder is in childhood, they are more likely to be physically aggressive, tend to have few, if any, friends, and when they reach adulthood are more likely to have antisocial personality disorder. Teenagers diagnosed with adolescent-onset conduct disorders are less aggressive, generally have few friends but they are less likely to become antisocial personalities as adults. However, they may become valued gang members. One problem with conduct disorder is that many juveniles go undiagnosed and grow into problem adults or they commit extremely violent crimes while young.

Abusive Parents

Parents should be authoritative with children. Each child needs rules to follow to learn self-discipline and to know that the rules are there because parents love them and want to help them develop. Authoritative parents using this style will rely on a combination of expert, informational, reward, and coercive methods and research indicates the authoritative style is effective.

Authoritarian parents may be cold and unloving and can cause a child to become resentful, angry, aggressive, and a discipline problem. Authoritarian parents tend to be harsh and punitive with the child and expect the child to follow their rules in a rigid manner. In some cases, authoritarian parents are physically abusive to a child to get the child to do what they want. Many times, the rules these parents make are not clear and the child does not know what to expect. The child can also act out his or her frustrations in a way that is not appropriate for society. The child of an authoritarian can be more aggressive with other children or can be a discipline problem in the classroom. The child can even take this a step further and act out frustrations in very violent actions because he or she has become indifferent to violent action.

Even children who come from homes that are not necessarily physically abusive but are psychologically abusive can act out their frustrations in an inappropriate manner. If the parents of a child do not get along and are constantly fighting with one another or even aggressive with one another, this can give a child the wrong idea about how to deal with other people. Family tension can heighten the aggressive behaviors of a child and in some cases, it might be better for the child to have only one parent rather two who have constant tension of some sort. However, a marital breakup can cause a child great disturbance and the potential to become aggressive. Parents who reject children cause a great deal of pain for the child and this can have an effect on whether or not the child becomes aggressive.

Parents who are permissive or indulgent do not communicate rules clearly to their child nor do they enforce what they do communicate. This can also cause the child to become resistant, aggressive, impulsive and low in self-control.

Inept Parents

According to learning theory, antisocial behavior is influenced by the kind of models the parents provide. Some parents can be classified as inept as role models for children. They don't have the ability to be effective parents. They are likely to allow the members of their family to interact in ways that reinforce their children's aggressive behavior. They may further provoke their children's ineffective conduct by being harsh and punitive to a greater degree than necessary. Gerald Patterson of the Oregon Social Learning Center found there are important parental functions that inept parents do not practice, possibly because they don't know how because they never learned:

1. They don't effectively monitor the activities of their children both inside and outside of the home.
2. They fail to discipline antisocial behavior adequately.
3. They don't reward prosocial conduct sufficiently.
4. They are not good at problem-solving.

Inept parents may be following the same pattern that their parents followed. Their ineptness was learned from their parents who learned it from their parents.

Stress

It is sometimes difficult to realize that children might be subject to an inordinate amount of stress. As with adults, there are innumerable circumstances that create increasing amounts of stress on young people at home, in social situations, at school, or at work. Most children may be able to handle the stress they are subjected to but there are some who do not do well and the stress may cause them to react in a manner that is inappropriate, such as fighting, belligerence, or perhaps lethal violence. Several of the students who committed violent acts in school were thought to be depressed and oversensitive to others. Some of these symptoms are directly related to stress and the inability to cope with stress.

Lack of Conflict Resolution Skills

All people, including young people, have a point at which they lose their tempers. They need not be mentally ill or unstable to aggravate a relationship or resort to violence. Even the most meek person will at one point fight back. There are proven techniques and processes of positive conflict resolution, but there are too few people who possess them and these skills are often not taught to children. Also, if the conflict resolution skills of parents are not effective the child will not learn how to resolve conflict successfully in the home.

Media Influence

If a child does not know how to successfully resolve a conflict situation he or she may become frustrated and angry at his or her inability to solve disputes. One way to learn about resolving conflict is from books, movies, computer games, or music. The alarming fact is that in many of these media, conflict is often resolved in a violent manner. If a young person does not realize this is fantasy or has some psychological problems and connects what he sees, reads, or hears to real life, he may get the idea that he can resolve conflict in the same manner. In most of the cases of school violence, the perpetrator has been suspected of being significantly influenced by some type of media.

Another fact about the media is that it may desensitize young people to violence. Although media specialists and the public in general believe that there is only a minor negative influence on children, there have been a number of studies to the contrary on the media's influence on aggressive acts. Some critics of the media claim that the constant exposure to violence legitimizes its use in the minds of those who were never introduced to positive behavioral responses.

In looking at the media's influence, the Internet must also be considered as an influence if not a cause. Several of the young people who have committed school violence have learned how to make bombs from the Internet. There are also several gang sites and hate sites that are an influence on the way that young people think, and the Internet is not censored which makes all sites accessible. Many young people have the ability to access the Internet at home.

Substance Abuse

Although there has been little evidence to substantiate that any of those who committed school violence were addicted to or taking illegal drugs, some of them were found to be taking prescription drugs for different psychological problems. The introduction of any chemical substance into the body and mind can have a devastating effect on one's perceptions and thought processes whether the substsance is legal or illegal. Thinking, moods, and behavior are rendered unpredictable. Prescription drugs sometimes have unpredictable side effects if they are taken improperly or mixed with other drugs. Even caffeine, found in most soft drinks, is suspected of influencing moods.

Mental Disorders

Michael Carneal pleaded guilty but mentally ill to the school shooting in West Paducah, KY, which raises the question about mental illness playing an important factor in school violence. The source of mental illness is still being argued by experts. Some say it is inherited; others claim it is caused by environmental influences; and still others claim it is a result of chemical imbalances in the body. It is probably rooted in all of these theories and whatever the cause, it is common and, as stated earlier, there is no reason to believe that young people suffer less from mental illness than do adults.

Mental disorders may be the genesis of some violent behavior but more often they are an aggravating factor. When young people are undergoing significant and persistent frustration, they will attempt to unload it in some manner. One way to do this is to turn the frustration inwardly against themselves. This may cause the manifestations of psychophysiologic disorders such as:

- Somatic or body function disorders related to eating or sleeping
- Headaches
- Weight loss or gain

Another way to unload frustration is by taking it out on an inanimate object. The most dangerous way of venting frustrations is on other people. If a mentally ill student perceives that other students are antagonizing him by teasing or degrading him, he may choose to vent their frustrations on them.

A Cycle of Violence

Psychologist John Monahan has developed a model that probably best describes the mental and behavioral responses and the set of circumstances that over time may escalate into a violent reaction. This generic model may best describe the processes that a potentially violent student might go through before he commits a violent act:

- The cycle begins when a student encounters an event that he considers stressful. What one person does not consider stressful another person will. The stressful event may be a perceived insult, threat or annoyance by a teacher or another student. Most of the recent violent acts in schools seemed to be triggered by teasing, insults, or rejection by girlfriends.
- The student reacts to the event with certain kinds of thoughts to which he is predisposed by his personality. A potentially violent student may start thinking of ways that he can get back at the people who he considers have been his antagonists.
- These thoughts lead to emotional responses. Emotions like empathy or guilt can inhibit a student from becoming violent. Emotional reactions that may lead the student to become violent are anger, hate and blame. Students who react in this manner are more likely to escalate to violence at some point in time. A student does not have to become highly emotional to become violent and in many cases, may be very calm when committing the violent act.
- These responses in turn determine the behavior that the student will use to respond to the situation. At this stage of the model, the student may decide to respond in one of two ways, withdraw and avoid, or fight. The student may think the only way to deal with the situation is to use physical violence.

The cycle continues as other people in the student's environment respond to his behavior in a way that will increase or decrease the student's stress. If the environment increases the student's stress, the reactive thoughts and emotions he has are likely to be intensified. These emotions can reach a point where the student believes that the best way to cope is violence. The responses to the student by others around them, such as parents, teachers, and other students as well as the media can have a de-escalating or escalating effect on the student and possibly push him or her over the edge. School violence is never a sudden event (as evidenced by the year-long planning of Harris and Klebold) and the student usually gives frequent and repeated warnings that he is going to be violent.

Profile of a Potentially Violent Student

No absolute characteristics are common to all violent students. However, there are certain traits and behaviors that are typical among students who do become violent. Creating a profile of a potentially violent student may be misleading. Such a definitive profile might be too exclusive and possibly dangerous. A description of a typical violent student is merely a composite average of a random group of students who have been known to commit a violent act at school. The fact that a student does fit the profile might cause other students and teachers to treat this person in an alienating manner that could lead to a self-fulfilling prophecy. Such false fears could cause a negative reaction in schools creating problems where none exist. At the same time, to ignore the behavior typologies of a potentially violent student could be a serious or fatal oversight.

The general profile of a potentially violent student might be:

- *Male* — Although all of the cases of school shootings investigated by the authors have been perpetrated by males, this does not mean that females can be totally excluded from the possibility of committing a violent act.
- *Between the ages of 11–18* — Although younger students have brought weapons to school, most have not used them. However, in Indianapolis, IN, a second-grader did point a gun at a classmate but the gun misfired.
- *A loner* — This is a student who does not have many friends or is labeled as "different" by other students, and is ridiculed or taunted for these perceived differences. Other students at school would probably describe him as a person who keeps to himself or as an introvert. Others may perceive him as being aloof, and he will develop his own values and habits that usually are quite different from other students. He may also be hypersensitive to criticism from other students who will hurt his feelings without knowing it. He will probably not show his hurt externally but will internalize it, with each episode building resentment toward the ones who hurt him. He may have an unrealistic concept of justice, perceiving that others are not being punished for what they do to him and he must exact justice himself. He may also

have few relationships (such as a girlfriend) and may become very upset if a relationship ends.

- *A fascination for weapons of all sorts.* The student may associate weapons with power and heroics. He may carry a weapon on a regular basis to school or to other functions for protection. He may also find a fascination in building and exploding bombs.
- *A fascination with killing.* This student makes a point of telling other classmates of his fascination or makes a suggestion that he might kill for revenge.
- *Past conduct problems or problems with authority.* The student may have problems with parents. He or she may be very combative, have a short temper and have used intimidation to get things that he or she wants.
- *Influenced by cults, cult music, or heavy metal, and rap music.* He or she may follow a cult or music that suggests violence and aggression are appropriate methods of "getting even."
- *Problems with drugs and alcohol.*
- *Cruelty to animals.* He or she may have beaten or killed an animal. Luke Woodham killed his dog before his murder spree.
- *Excessive stress in the home such as the divorce of parents.*
- *Problems with depression.* He may feel helplessness or powerlessness against others. He may feel that others control his destiny and that whatever happens to him in life is caused by external conditions (this may be a concern for the potential of student suicide).

At one time or another, probably every student may fit into one or more of the categories in the profile, but any one of these categories is only a guideline, not an absolute.

4 Strategies for Reducing/Preventing School Violence

S chool administrators and teachers have legal and moral obligations in both violence prevention and student protection. All schools must take steps to ensure a safe and healthful learning environment for children. To ensure this, school administrators and teachers must be both proactive and re-active. They must have plans to prevent or reduce school violence and plans to implement if school violence happens. Administrators must also face the fact that they cannot overreact or underreact to situations, but they must handle situations in an appropriate manner that is beneficial to the students and the school. No one knows whether school mass killings can be totally prevented but it is necessary to try any measures that might keep them from happening.

In looking at all of the school violence that has occurred in the U.S., it is easy to see the possibilities of a school mass-killing are small but they are high profile situations. The fact that the odds are small leads to one of the problems that school administrators, teachers, and even parents seem to have—denial that violence could happen in their school. One of the first statements to be heard from people involved in any type of violence is, "We didn't think it could happen here." It can happen anywhere anytime and each school must be prepared to prevent the situation from happening or ready to respond when a situation does happen. The first step toward preventing or reducing violence is to acknowledge the problem does exist or could exist in the future.

Although there may be no indicators upon which school officials can rely to indicate *exactly* when a student is going to become violent, several behavioral typologies of violent students have been set forth in this book to alert officials to the potentials of student violence. Many times, potentially violent students will give a warning by their actions indicating they are planning to do something. In the case of Springfield, OR, the student was not only sent home from school for possession of a weapon, but many students were also aware that he could potentially be violent. Every precaution should have been made to ensure that student never entered the building the next day.

In other cases, students have made specific statements to other students of their intentions. This is either their warning to classmates or a cry for help that usually goes unheeded. Certainly, when these conditions exist, school administrators, teachers, or students should do something. Early intervention in many of these cases might have prevented an incident from happening, such as in Gas City, IN, where administrators found out about a potential incident that was to take place, and took steps to prevent it.

Obviously, the more information school officials have regarding the behavior of students, the better chance they have of predicting potential violent actions. According to forensic psychologist Shawn A. Johnston, "There is an evolving body of research that very clearly suggests by the third grade, we're able to identify kids who are at risk of engaging in antisocial aggression." That aggression predicts the potential for violence well into an individual's 30s in every culture in which it has been studied.

Teacher Involvement

Efforts to prevent violence in schools must involve teachers. All teachers should be aware of discipline problems, including any act of violence or threat of violence that has occurred in the school. Meetings should be held to apprise teachers of what is going on and what is expected of them. The more teachers know what is going on in the school, the more help they will be in the solution. Teachers want a safe school and they should be an integral part of making the school safe.

Teachers should post the school behavior standards in the classroom. The teacher is responsible for establishing and maintaining the climate in the classroom and for managing the students. A teacher must establish control of the classroom the first day of school and then maintain it every day. Students are very perceptive and know quickly those teachers who are not in control of their classroom. Being in control does not mean being a "tyrant"; it means asserting authority and demanding and getting respect. The classroom teacher must ensure the behavior and academic standards of the school are followed. Some methods of creating a motivating and peaceful classroom are:

■ Demonstrate a genuine interest in students by treating students as individuals. Offer praise and encouragement when warranted.

- Communicate all classroom rules clearly to all students.
- Be objective with students, not judgmental. Look at matters from a student's point of view.
- Minimize the power differential between you and students. Get out from behind the desk or podium.
- Address any behavior problems directly and immediately so they will not expand.
- Use a collaborative approach by soliciting students' opinions.
- Demonstrate you are human by using humor and/or admitting to your mistakes.

Many times, teachers see the negative behavior of a student long before the student reacts violently. Teachers are often unprepared to address a disruptive or violent student. Teachers must receive intensive training and staff development for dealing with discipline and violence.

Threat Reporting

Since most of the children who engage in mass killings have given previous warnings, at least to fellow students, a threat reporting system should be set up for all schools. There should be rules that *all students and parents* are aware of that will allow any student or parent to report a threat of any kind either to a teacher, administrator, or to a hotline. If students know they can report the threat anonymously to a hotline, they may be more likely to report it. Once the threat has been reported, the student making the report must be interviewed to determine:

- The exact nature of the threat.
- The specific circumstances in which the threat was made.
- The names of any other students who heard the threat or have knowledge of other threats that have been made by the student in the past.
- The need for an investigation to be conducted to determine the veracity of the threat report. The investigation should be conducted in a discreet manner; any interviews conducted with students must be kept confidential and thoroughly documented. There is always the possibility the student reporting the threat has done so to get back at another student.
- The severity of the threat. Sometimes this assessment is difficult to do. If there are questions about the severity and potential for realization, outside professional help should be consulted before final determinations are made as to what actions are required.

There is a note of caution in attempting to predict accurately the potential for violent behavior. In 1981, psychologist John Monahan, an expert on the prediction of violent behavior, stated, "All a person predicting violence can hope to do is assign a probability figure to the occurrence of violent behavior by a given individual during a given time period." If this is the case, the question is, "What does the assessed degree of probability recommend in the way of prevention?"

If there is sufficient probability to believe the threat is valid, a specific plan of action must be developed in response. If the threat is definitely valid:

1. The student(s) should be removed from school until other options can be developed.
2. The parents should be notified of the threat. Let them know if the student is potentially violent because they could be the first victims. Some parents may deny their child would make a threat and may not want to cooperate with school officials to monitor the student. If the parents do not cooperate, the school should still continue monitoring the student.
3. The school should be secured so the potential of the student(s) getting back in is reduced to as near zero as possible. This may include using law enforcement agencies.

If the threat is questionable but there is suspicion that it could be valid:

1. The movement of suspected students in and out of the school should be monitored carefully. The student(s) should not be allowed to leave the classroom except for an emergency.
2. School security and teachers would be used to help monitor.
3. Only those who will be responsible for helping to monitor the student(s) should know of the situation. Rumors travel rapidly in the school environment and if a student is not dangerous the rumor could damage the reputation of the student.

Such a plan must also include the protection of the student who has reported the threat. If the student making the threatening statements learns that another student has reported him, the student reporting the threat may also be in danger of retaliation outside of the school.

School Discipline

Every school system should have a clearly defined discipline code that is communicated to students, administrators, teachers, and parents each year. If legal in the state, there should be, on record, the signatures of these people to show they have received the discipline code.

Most discipline will be for corrective purposes rather than for punishment and should focus on helping the student correct negative behavior. Such discipline should be applied in a firm, fair, and consistent manner. Many times discipline is given in what students consider to be an unfair and inconsistent manner and in some situations, they may be correct. Teachers and administrators are no less human and often use emotion to determine a discipline penalty that is usually not objective. In some cases, administrators or teachers do not discipline because they are intimated by the student(s).

Some suggestions for the administration of positive corrective discipline are as follows:

1. Focus on the behavior of the student rather than on his or her character. Focusing on character may stimulate a negative emotional response. Remember the discipline is to change the student's behavior.
2. Do not let the disciplinary session with the student become an argument. Arguments almost always end with hard feelings on both sides and no lasting resolution to the problems.
3. Listen to the student's point of view. Active listening is an acquired skill similar to learning to be an effective speaker. Listening gives the student an opportunity to vent, to release pent-up frustrations. Skillful active listening, along with encouraging the student to explain the situation in detail and from different viewpoints, often will result in a better understanding of the situation.
4. Follow up with increased surveillance of the situation to make sure the student is correcting the behavior for which he was disciplined. If the student corrects the behavior, let him know that you appreciate the new behavior.

One of the complaints of administrators is that teachers do not administer discipline in a consistent manner. One of the complaints of teachers is that administrators do not support teachers when they report students for disruptive or violent behavior. Administrators must give teachers the support they need to maintain an orderly classroom. Nothing is more disheartening for a teacher than to send a student to the office for discipline, then the student returns to the classroom without anything being done. This has a negative effect on the relationship between the teacher and the student. The administrator does not investigate the student's behavior nor is the student disciplined for what he has done. Administrators must investigate the student's behavior and the teacher must be notified as to what action or nonaction will be taken and the reasons for the action before the student is allowed to return to the classroom.

Zero Tolerance

Some incidents are so serious they warrant punitive discipline. In such a case, the student should be suspended from school pending an investigation. Serious incidents can happen on school property ar at a school function off school property. Examples of incidents that warrant "zero tolerance" are:

- Possessing a dangerous weapon
- Drinking alcohol
- Using or dealing illegal drugs
- Possessing a prescription drug that is not for the student
- Fighting

For example, zero tolerance should apply to any student who brings a weapon to school. Such an action should bring, at the minimum, a suspension until all the facts are gathered. If warranted, the student should then be expelled and possibly prosecuted for possession of a weapon. However, a student who is suspended or expelled can become even more dangerous. Students who are suspended or expelled should not be allowed to return to school premises under *any* circumstances. Their daily activities should be monitored until action is taken by the court system or they are deemed to be nonthreats. Monitoring should last more than a day because the student could return at any time for vengeance.

5 | Security Procedures

I t is not the desire of anyone to have a school be an armed camp. This sends the wrong message to students or to anyone associated with the school. However, it is imperative that a school is safe and one of the ways to keep it safe is to have adequate security. Most schools that have been built in recent years were not built with security in mind, so this makes security procedures more important.

Monitoring Students

One of the most common school security measures used to prevent violence requires the school staff, administrators, teachers, and security staff (if available) to monitor students' movements in and around the school and where students congregate in large numbers. So far, this method of monitoring has not been successful in retarding the mass killings that have happened. Violence still happens every day in the halls of schools and teachers are sometimes so intimidated they refuse to monitor the halls. Most of the time violence that happens inside of the school is never reported to outside authorities.

General Security Procedures for Schools

Schools are notorious for easy access and students know all of the ins and outs of getting into a particular school. This makes security an even more difficult matter when trying to defend against a potential mass killing. Also, many schools built today are not built with security in mind. Although there is no one method of fail-safe security, the following general security items must be considered:

- School officials should consider the possibility of using metal detectors and randomly searching students entering a building—specifically, any student suspected of possession of a weapon. When new schools are built or old ones remodeled, metal detectors can be built into the door frames.

■ Once the school day has started, all doors to the school should be locked to entrance from the outside except for one door. Anyone coming into the school after school starts should have to come through that one door and it should be monitored with a metal detector.

■ Visitors to the school should be required to sign in at the office and given visitors' passes. They must also be escorted to where they are going in the building and not allowed to roam the building at will.

■ There should be plain signs on all doors telling visitors to report to the office.

■ A security officer at the door must detain anyone setting off the metal detector.

■ If a student has been identified as a potential problem, such as making a threat, that student should be monitored very closely every day.

■ Students who have been identified as potentially aggressive should be monitored closely.

■ Each school should have a security person(s), depending on the size of the school, present every day. Some large school systems have their own security force. In several of the schools that have suffered shootings, there were no security personnel in the building. Some small schools may feel that they don't need security but in most cases, it would be wise to have at least part-time security during the time when students are moving between classes or before school when students congregate.

■ Schools should be secured after school hours or when school activities are complete (someone could plant a bomb after hours if there is access to the school).

■ If possible, have custodians in the school all night. Don't have a custodian work alone; have at least two of them.

■ Put silent panic alarms in the offices and classrooms to summon help if needed.

■ Put telephones or two-way radios in classrooms to report problems.

■ Every school should conduct a semi-annual school safety assessment. The safety assessment should include the following items:
— An evaluation of the school safety plan and the planning process.
— An assessment of the school/law enforcement partnership.
— A review of policies and procedures.
— An assessment of weapons in school.

— An assessment of drug and alcohol use in school.

— An assessment of student attitudes and motivation.

— An assessment of the crisis management plan.

— An assessment of violent activities in the school.

■ Security cameras should be installed at doors and where students congregate in numbers. The cameras should remain on all the time to tape activities. These cameras can be mounted in a manner that is not intrusive for students.

■ All school buses on school property should be locked at all times and parked behind a locked fence.

■ Bulletproof glass should be installed in all glass located inside of the building. This would help to ensure the safety of students in rooms and for school officials in the main office.

■ Office doors and classroom doors should be metal and should be able to be locked from the inside.

■ Practice crisis drills should be conducted for all school staff.

6 The Crisis Management Team and Crisis Plan

In addition to taking steps to reduce or prevent potential violence, a plan must be created for action when violence does occur. A crisis management team (CMT) and a crisis planning center should be created to develop a crisis plan for each specific school location in a school system. Some school systems may even have a separate planning team to develop a crisis management plan. Generally, the people who create the plan, the CMT, are more likely to make the plan work.

The crisis plan should include one specific telephone number in each superintendent's or principal's office to receive all reports of threats, intimidation, altercations, and potentially violent students. The plan should create the rules and regulations concerning the reporting requirements of students, the prohibitions against making threats, harassing or intimidating students, or exhibiting violence of any kind, and the sanctions for violations of the rules and regulations. The plan must create specific action plans and appropriate guidelines for the proactive and reactive responses to any events. The plan must be put in written form and distributed to all school personnel.

The CMT should consist of:

■ The school system superintendent. Although the superintendent may not be located in the school building(s), he or she should still be part of the CMT for planning purposes
■ The building principal
■ The building assistant principal
■ Maintenance (absolutely necessary for their knowledge of the building and its equipment)
■ School security personnel and law enforcement personnel

- Any other person deemed necessary for effective handling of a crisis situation, such as:
  — School board member(s)
  — Legal counsel
  — Media relations person
  — Teachers (preferably with experience in crisis situations)
  — Parent of a student
- Each school building (if the school system has multiple buildings) should have a CMT and crisis management plan

A crisis management plan should consist of:

1. CMT information, including:
   - Phone numbers of the CMT (home and school).
   - Phone numbers of any agencies or people who should be notified of a crisis or potential crisis situation (a telephone calling tree to notify the Crisis Response Team (CRT) if different from the CMT).
   - Location of the crisis center in each building. This could be a room from which chairs can be removed or grouped to satisfy the needs of the situation.
   - Immediate responses of the CMT should a crisis occur.
   - Who does what and when?
2. Identification of potential crisis situations, including:
   - What incidents should be considered crisis situations.
   - A crisis situation is any situation that is not part of the normal school experience:
     — Bomb threat (Note Appendix for form to be used in case of a bomb threat.)
     — Shooting
     — Suicide or attempted suicide by a student
     — Fire
     — Other situations that potentially could cause harm to students and/or faculty, such as bad weather
     — Who designates an incident as a crisis and how people are to be informed of the crisis (fire alarm, intercom, etc.) In the case of a shooting, there may be no opportunity to appoint someone to designate a crisis situation.

3. Identification of security/emergency needs:
   ■ For each situation, these needs should be identified:
     — Law enforcement
     — Medical
     — Fire
     — Psychological (counseling intervention team for students, teachers, administrators, and parents)
   ■ The person(s) responsible for notifying these agencies.
4. Media contact plan, including:
   ■ When media gets involved, who interacts with them and who does not. One person should be designated as the media contact person and no one else should talk to the media.
5. Emergency procedures, including:
   ■ Evacuation plans (fire, bomb threat, and violent weather drills should be practiced and enforced on a regular basis. However, this should be done with extreme care and planning because of the incident in Jonesboro, AR). The evacuation plan for each room and office should be posted in that room or office in a place that can be easily seen. The faculty member/administrator responsible for the room or office should be completely familiar with the plan and should communicate the plan to anyone who uses the room or office.
   ■ Plans for a bomb or other type of terrorist threat.
   ■ Lists of personnel and their functions in an emergency situation (in addition to the CMT, such as the CRT).
6. Location of equipment and shutoff valves/switches.
   ■ Valves and switches for gas, oil, water, and electricity.
   ■ Location of emergency and protective equipment.
   ■ Location of tools.
7. First aid training.
   ■ A significant number, preferably all, school officials (administrators, teachers, maintenance) should be trained in first aid and cardiopulmonary resuscitation (CPR).
8. All administration, faculty, and students should be made aware of the crisis management plan and each person's role in the plan. They should know:
   ■ Where evacuation plans are posted and understand the evacuation plan.

- ■   What to do when a crisis has been designated.
- ■   How a specific crisis will be designated.

9. The CMT should meet frequently to review crisis plans and assess the readiness for a crisis.

After *any crisis situation,* the CMT should meet to evaluate how the crisis was handled.

7 Specific Emergency Procedures for Schools

Intruder Response

If a person enters the building and does not follow the visitor procedure, he or she might be someone who is acting upset, emotional, or carrying some type of weapon. Intruders should not be approached by students or faculty. The first person to identify an intruder should notify the principal's office by the quickest method (walkie-talkie, phone, or direct contact) to report:

- The intruder's location
- The intruder's description
- The number of intruders
- The direction the intruder is headed in the building
- Whether or not the intruder possesses a weapon

The principal or her or his representative should sound a preplanned alarm that all teachers and administrations will understand, such as: "Attention everyone, the visitors have arrived. Please prepare for them."

The alarm will mean:

- All classroom doors will be locked immediately and lights will be turned off. The classroom door should not be opened for anyone.
- No student should be allowed to leave the classroom.
- Each teacher should take an accurate count of students.
- All students in the halls will go immediately to the nearest classroom.

- Teachers and students should position themselves along the interior walls of the classroom away from windows and doors.
- The intruder will be monitored by designated administrators or security personnel.
- If the intruder is identified as dangerous or potentially dangerous, law enforcement should be summoned immediately.
- The school superintendent's office will be notified.
- A designated administrator should meet with law enforcement when they arrive, outside of the school with a school map to pinpoint as nearly as possible the location of the intruder.
- Once an intruder situation has been resolved, an announcement can be made that it is "all clear" and students and teachers will be allowed to leave the classrooms.

Hostage Situations

In more than one instance of school violence, students and/or teachers have been held hostage in the schools. A case in point is the situation in Moses Lake, WA, where the student held his algebra class hostage and then killed two students and a teacher. Hostages can be taken and held for significant periods of time. Hostage negotiations must be conducted by law enforcement officers trained to do so. However, in every school building, there should be at least one or two teachers or administrators trained in hostage negotiations to stabilize the situation until law enforcement arrives. The student may also be more inclined to talk with a teacher than with law enforcement.

A hostage situation is different from an intruder situation. In some cases, school officials may overreact. Once a hostage situation has been identified, the following procedures should be followed.

- Call law enforcement immediately and let them know there is a hostage situation at the school.
- The principal or his or her designated representative should sound a preplanned alarm (different from the intruder alarm so teachers and administrators will know that it is a hostage situation, such as, "Attention all educators, the visitors have arrived in the (room number or area). Please prepare for them."
- Classrooms should be locked and lights turned out and students should sit along an inside wall. No student or teacher will be allowed to leave the classroom.

- Designated school personnel should monitor hallways to direct students to a safe area.
- All students should be accounted for by teachers.
- A predetermined person should be assigned as liaison with law enforcement to provide as much information as is known, such as names of persons holding hostages and names of persons being held.
- When the situation has been resolved, an "all clear" announcement should be made over the intercom.
- The CMT should prepare a statement for the staff and students.

If students and/or teachers are taken hostage, there are no behaviors that guarantee survival. Also, it may not be feasible to train every student in how to react in a hostage situation but it is possible to train teachers and administrators in what to do in a hostage situation to increase the odds of survival:

- Do not argue with the hostage-taker over any issue, particularly about his behavior or the reasons for it.
- Do not separate or set yourself against him. Even though you might feel this way, the more closely you can relate to his situation, the better chance you have of surviving.
- Encourage him to talk, and be sympathetic with him, listening to what he has to say. If he identifies his target(s), sympathize with his viewpoint.
- Do not try to reason with him, to defend yourself or what has happened to him. You probably will be better off agreeing with him on what has happened. Do not tell him that you understand how he feels, because he knows that you don't.
- Do not be condescending in any way. He may only be a young boy but he has the power, and condescension at this point could be fatal.
- Do not give him the impression you think he will fail or that it is hopeless for him to succeed. At this time, he is the master of your fate.
- Make him think that you are submitting to his control and you are at his mercy. Don't make it appear you are on guard.
- Side with him on all matters. Remember, as a teacher or administrator, you may have not only yourself to think of but also there may be several students he is holding hostage. Your objective is to get them and yourself out of the situation alive.

Bomb Threat

Any bomb threat to a school must be considered real and dangerous. If a bomb threat is received during school hours, the following procedure should be followed.

- Whoever answers the call should prolong the conversation as long as possible to get as much information as possible and try to take the message down exactly as it was delivered.
- The person receiving the call will notify the principal immediately.
- Evacuate the school by using the fire drill procedure.
- Call law enforcement, notifying them of a bomb threat.
- Do not touch anything or open any containers.
- Notify the school superintendent's office.
- A designated person will be assigned to meet with law enforcement, outside of the building, to give them a map and report anything out of the ordinary.
- If the search is to be long or the weather is inclement, students and teachers should be relocated to another area.
- When the search is concluded and the building is safe, the daily schedule can be resumed.
- If a bomb threat is received in writing, all of the procedures should be followed and the original message should be preserved for law enforcement to attempt to identify its sender.

Shots-Fired Procedure

There may be a situation where shots are actually fired in the building. If this is the situation:

- If it is at all possible, someone should make an announcement over the PA system that "Shots have been fired."
- If shots are fired in the building, it must be assumed that many students and teachers will panic and not attempt to follow any procedure or even remember what procedure to follow. It is imperative that law enforcement and emergency personnel get to the school as quickly as possible.
- Anyone who can do so should call law enforcement immediately, even if it results in multiple calls.

- If there has been a warning, all classrooms should be locked and lights turned off and students should be against the inside wall.
- A shooter will probably try to fire shots at a time and place where there are the most students present.
- If students and teachers exit the building, they should not be allowed to return under any circumstances and they should be taken to a safe area.
- When law enforcement arrives, they will be in charge.

School Functions

There may be a situation where a crisis arises at a school function. The chaperones or whoever is in charge of that particular function must be prepared to handle the crisis and protect all attending the function:

- School dance, on school property:
  — Before the dance, the persons chaperoning the dance should meet and develop a plan if the dance should have to be evacuated.
  — It may be necessary to have plain-clothed law enforcement officers at the dance.
- School dance, off school property:
  — Before the dance, the persons in charge of chaperoning the dance should meet with officials of the facility hosting the dance to discuss safety plans and evacuation procedures in case of a crisis situation.
- Other school functions:
  — For any school function, such as basketball games, there needs to be a crisis plan developed before the function and the persons responsible for the function will be responsible for implementing the plan if necessary.
  — After all school functions, on school property, someone needs to be designated to check all doors, etc., in the building to make sure everything is secure.
- School functions at other schools:
  — School administration is responsible for meeting with other schools to review their crisis management plans before an away school function is held.

Student Searches

A search of a student or his or her property is a very serious matter and should be done with extreme care. The Fourth Amendment to the U.S. Constitution protects a student from unreasonable search by public school officials on school property, school buses, and at school events. Additionally, each state may have laws or guidelines concerning school searches and if those do exist, they should be referred to before any search of a student is made. If there is any question in the legality of a specific student search, the administrators should contact their own school attorney or the local prosecutor for guidance. Also, if a school creates its own search policy, the school attorney and local prosecutors should have a part in creating that policy.

General Guidelines for School Searches

- What is *not* a search:
  - Observing an object after the student has denied ownership of that object.
  - Observing an object that has been abandoned by a student.
  - Observing any object that is in plain view, exposed to the public.
  - Detecting and/or observing anything that is exposed to the senses of sight, smell, or hearing as long as the school official(s) are located in a position where they have a right to be and were not using unusual means to gain a vantage point.
- What is a search:
  - Opening and inspecting a student's personal possessions.
  - Physically examining or patting down a student's body and clothing including pockets.
  - Examining places that are not open to public view.
  - Using extraordinary means to enlarge the ability to view into closed, locked areas.
  - It is not advisable to use the type of search known as a "strip search" because federal courts have found them to be unreasonable.

To conduct a search, a school official or a school security officer must have "reasonable grounds" (reasonable grounds means there is a suspicion based on reasons that can be articulated, not a mere hunch or supposition) to believe all of the following:

- A criminal law or school policy rule has been or is being violated.
- A specific student has violated a criminal law or school rule.
- The suspected criminal law or school rule violation is a kind for which there may be physical evidence.

- The sought-after evidence would be found in a particular place associated with the student suspected of violating a criminal law or school rule.
- Some reasonable grounds that justify a search:
  — Observation of a criminal law or school rule violation in progress.
  — Observation of a weapon.
  — Observation of items that are believed to be stolen.
  — Smell of burning tobacco or marijuana.
  — The student appears to be under the influence of alcohol or drugs.
  — The student admits to a criminal law or a school rule violation.
  — The student makes a threat in words or behavior.
  — Emergency situations, where school officials can provide immediate assistance to avoid serious injury.
  — Oral or written consent by the student that is not gained by fear, duress, or intimidation.
- General guidelines for a student search:
  — *Never* search a student in the presence of another student.
  — Take the student to a private area.
  — Closely observe the student so he or she doesn't discard anything.
  — The search must be for the suspected item involved in a criminal law or school rule violation.
  — Have a third-party present (the same sex as the student to avoid charges of improper conduct by the person doing the search).
  — Tell the student what you suspect he has and give him an opportunity to surrender the suspected item.
  — If any item that violates criminal laws or school rules is found, the item must be seized.
  — Place the item in an envelope.
  — Identify the item in the envelope with date and time seized.
  — Name the persons present when the item was seized.
  — Secure the envelope in a locked area.

Student Fights

There are times when a fight will erupt between or among students. It is difficult for faculty to know what to do but there are some guidelines:

- The first priority for a school employee is to avoid getting hurt.
  — If possible, the teacher should send another student for help or use a walkie-talkie, if available, to call for assistance.

- Deal with the fighters.
  - If you know their names call them out in a loud strong voice telling them to stop.
  - Keep a safe distance from the fight.
  - If your voice does not work, try a loud noise such as clapping your hands.
- Once the fight has stopped, you want to disband the crowd of students.
  - Tell the students to leave and go to their next class.
  - Do not scream but use a loud, strong voice.

Use of Physical Force by a School Employee

Physical force may be used by a school employee against a student as long as the force is reasonable, moderate, and necessary to maintain order or prevent a student from harming herself or himself, other students, school staff, or school property and there is no other reasonable effective alternative. In the case of a school employee using force against a student to protect a third party, the facts, as they appear to the protector, must create a reasonable expectation that the third party is in imminent danger and about to be injured.

- The force must not exceed what would be justified in the person protecting himself.
- The employee must believe that intervention is absolutely necessary to protect the third party.

There may be different laws in states as to use of physical force by a school employee. If you have a question as to the use of physical force in your state, contact the state attorney general to find out the appropriate laws.

Events Involving Deaths

Another incident that will involve the need for a specific plan is the death of someone connected with the school. The following steps should be followed if a death happens:

- Death of a student.
  - Obtain the facts concerning the death.
  - Notify the principal and/or school superintendent.

— Notify the building CMT and they should decide on a time and place for a faculty/staff meeting.

1. The school principal initiates the telephone calling tree to all faculty and support staff informing them of the death and requesting their arrival at school at least 30 minutes early to attend a special faculty/staff meeting.

2. Sensitivity to the staff reaction should be considered when making the calls. Some of the staff may need some special support because they were close to the deceased student.

3. If appropriate notify any person who may have a special relationship with the deceased student, for example, a best friend. If a student falls into that category, his or her parents should be notified and given suggestions as to how they can provide support at home. If it is not possible to give such students notice before they arrive at school, they should be taken aside and notified privately as soon as they arrive at school.

4. Counselors should be contacted to be ready to assist students, teachers and administrators in their shock and grief.

5. The CMT should develop a plan for the day and coordinate efforts with the wishes of the family. The principal should conduct the faculty/staff meeting before school advising them of these plans. At the faculty/staff meeting, materials about the following should be available:
   — Phases of grieving
   — Factors influencing grief reactions
   — Normal vs. pathological grief
   — Tips for teachers
   — Memorials

6. The principal should announce a process/debriefing meeting for the faculty/staff to be held at the end of the day. At this meeting, specific concerns can be expressed and at-risk students can be identified for follow-up.

7. The principal should secure the personal belongings of the deceased and remove his or her name from the computer mailing list.

8. Provide areas for the students and staff to meet with counselors to discuss their feelings and concerns.

— When announcement to the student body is necessary:

9. Over the public address system, the principal will tell the entire student body to stay in their classrooms and to wait for instructions. Teachers and aides should be aware that they need to cooperate and keep students in class until instructed differently.

10. One or more persons (preferably the CMT members) should go to each class to convey the news of the event. If the school is very large, classroom teachers may have to make the announcement for the sake of time. All of the available information will be given in a calm, direct manner.

11. If available, information on funeral arrangements should be given.

12. When all of the classes have been informed, the principal should follow-up with a general announcement.

13. Announce to all students that counselors are available for them. Each teacher should get the names of students who are interested or appear to need to talk to someone.

14. The principal and counselors should conduct a process or debriefing meeting at the end of the day for the staff of the school to:
    — Allow for expressions of feelings and support
    — Review the events of the day
    — Determine which students might need further help
    — Determine the needs and plan for the next day

15. The CMT should conduct a process meeting for all faculty/staff at the end of one week after the crisis to:
    — Evaluate the actions and reactions to the event
    — Revise the procedures

■ Guidelines in responding to student suicide:
    — Follow the general format for death of a student.
    — When planning how to announce a suicide, remember that the emotions aroused by a suicide are more complex than by any other form of death. Containing these intense feelings is imperative for retaining control. With this heightened emotional state will come distortion of the facts; rumors generated are usually graphic and more gruesome than the actual event. Be sure of the facts because the death may only be a suspected suicide. Information given should be factual and not graphic. The deceased should neither be glorified nor vilified.
    — There is a potential for a single suicide in a school to trigger suicide

clusters. Therefore the aftermath of a suicide must be handled with expertise and understanding. Anxiety is especially rampant after a young person has committed suicide; all intense emotional reactions are amplified by having so many people in one place who are survivors.

■ Exceptions to the general format.
— It may not be advisable to hold a memorial service in response to a suicide because the service tends to dramatize and glorify the deceased and the suicidal act.
— School and community persons must be on the alert for additional suicide attempts within the teen population. All high-risk students must be identified. In the case of adolescent suicide clusters, these are the students who may be at risk:
  1. Relatives and/or close friends of the deceased
  2. Boy/girl friend of the deceased
  3. Pallbearers at the funeral
  4. Students absent in the following week, if clearly not for illness
  5. Students with a history of depression
  6. Students with weak social supports
  7. Students with known family troubles
  8. Any student involved in past suicidal attempts

■ Suicide or attempted suicide in school.
— Call 911 immediately and inform them of the situation and ask for law enforcement and emergency medical personnel.
— Isolate the area of the incident and students and/or faculty should not be allowed near the area unless a faculty member is needed for emergency medical treatment. It should be announced over the intercom that all students and faculty are to stay in the rooms they are in until they are released. Make sure teachers understand that if a bell sounds they are still to remain in the room even if the bell is to dismiss school. No one (students in particular) should leave a classroom until the incident has been handled by emergency personnel.
— Take student or faculty witnesses to an area where they can receive immediate counseling and then be interviewed by law enforcement.
— Notify counselors to come to the school immediately.
— Notify students a medical emergency has occurred and is being handled by emergency personnel.
— The suicide response guidelines should be followed if the incident is a confirmed suicide.
— School could be dismissed if the CMT deems it necessary.

- Death of a school staff member.
  — The CMT should call a meeting to inform faculty and staff of the death and to plan for an intervention. If the death occurs after school, the telephone calling tree can be utilized to request faculty and staff to arrive at school at a predetermined time for a meeting.
  — Information on the death can be given at the meeting and the faculty and staff can be given time to express their feelings and lend support to one another. If necessary, substitute teachers may be used for faculty who need them.
  — At the beginning of the day, each teacher can announce the death to her or his students and give them the basic facts. Students can be told they will be excused from classes to attend the funeral (with parental permission) and funeral arrangements will be announced as soon as they are available. An announcement can be made at this time that counselors are available.
  — The CMT will conduct a process and debriefing meeting at the end of the day to allow for the expression of feelings and to determine the needs for the next day.
- Death of a student's parent, sibling, or other close family member while the student is at school.
  — The death should be verified (via the parent, hospital, sheriff) and confirmed with the principal of the building.
  — Inform the student's teachers of the incident.
  — Determine who should tell the child (either a relative or school staff member).
  — If a school staff member is selected, make sure it is someone the student trusts.
  — The student should be taken to a place where he or she has privacy and will be able to rest.
  — The student should be told simply and directly. Avoid using platitudes and unnecessary details. The person should answer questions honestly and directly.
  — The person giving the student the news should remain with the student until a parent or guardian arrives.

8 The Aftermath of a Violent Situation

Although school violence, especially a shooting, is not a pleasant subject, it must be addressed and a plan must be in place for the aftermath. The following are actions for such a plan:

1. Obviously, the first consideration is to provide medical attention.
2. Suspend classes for a reasonable time. However, the school can be kept open so students, parents, teachers, etc., can come for counseling, unless the crisis situation forces the closure of the school indefinitely, such as in Littleton, CO. If this happens have a location designated for counseling.
3. Provide for immediate counseling for all students, teachers, etc., who wish to accept it. Contact the community crisis center that has been designated by the CMT for intervention in such a situation.

There can be major psychological trauma for students and/or teachers who witness or have been a part of the violence. Many people who suffer significant psychological trauma develop post-traumatic stress disorder (PTSD). Those who receive early counseling are better equipped to deal with PTSD and work through the stages of it more quickly. According to the *Diagnostic and Statistical Manual of Mental Disorders-IV (DSM-IV)*, a person with PTSD has been exposed to a traumatic event in which both of the following were present:

1. The person experienced, witnessed, or was confronted with an event or events that involved actual or threatened death or serious injury, or a threat to the physical integrity of self or others.
2. The person's response involved intense fear, helplessness, or horror.

In PTSD, the following symptoms are common:

1. The traumatic event is persistently re-experienced.
2. Persistent avoidance of stimuli associated with the trauma.
3. Persistent symptoms of increased arousal (not present before the trauma), as indicated by at least two of the following:
   — Difficulty falling asleep or staying asleep
   — Irritability or outburst of anger
   — Difficulty concentrating
   — Hypervigilance
   — An exaggerated startle response
   — A psychological activity when exposed to events that symbolize or resemble an aspect of the trauma

The PTSD is considered acute if the duration is less than three months and is considered chronic if the duration is longer that three months. For some individuals, the traumatic event remains for decades, in some instances for their whole lifetimes. It is a dominating psychological experience that has the power to evoke panic, terror, grief, or despair that will be manifested as daytime fantasies, nightmares, and flashbacks. Sufferers of PTSD may experience an effect known as "psychic numbing," and emotional anesthesia that makes it difficult for them to participate in meaningful interpersonal relationships.

Personal psychological counseling helps an individual to examine personal values and how he or she was violated during the traumatic event. The goal of the counseling is the resolution for the conscious and unconscious conflicts that were created by the event.

Research has indicated that of people who undergo traumatic events:

- One hundred percent of them have undergone major changes in either their lives or the lives of their families.
- Most victims feel vulnerable and unsafe after the violent experience.
- There are predictable phases of recovery that victims of violent experiences go through.
- The severity of the response to witnessing or experiencing violence is affected by the length of the incident and how much warning there was prior to the incident.

Media Procedures

The only method to inform the general public is by the mass media. Therefore it is important to ensure that the media receive prompt and accurate information.

One thing to remember is the media will be looking for anyone they can talk with or get a statement from, so isolated quotes from individuals can be incomplete or misleading and should be avoided. These guidelines should be followed:

- *Only* a person designated by the superintendent's office should give statements to the media.
- Refer all media contacts to the designated person.
- Do not talk with the media on the phone.
- Students and staff should not talk to the media.

Tips for interviews for the person designated to have contact with the media

1. Be honest. If you don't have the answer to a question say so. Don't make anything up because you feel pressured. Tell the media person you will get back with him or her with the answer as soon as you can. If you make a mistake in the interview, say so.
2. There is no such thing as "off the record."
3. If you are in a room with a microphone or camera, always assume it is on.
4. Try to have a goal for an interview. What do you want to accomplish?
5. Prepare for an interview. If you need time, ask for it.
6. Understand what you are going to say so you can talk about the topic knowledgeably.
7. Anticipate the worst question you may have to answer and plan for that in advance.
8. Bridge a question from where you are in the interview to where you want to be.
9. Never say, "No comment." It makes you sound as if you have something to hide.
10. Don't use jargon. You won't have a translator.

Guidelines for Emergency Notification

Following a crisis, send letters to the homes of all students that include the following:

1. The nature of the crisis and the basic facts.
2. Information about the utilization of the school crisis plan and the community's resources.

3. Description of the emotional reactions a student might exhibit.

4. A statement that the parents should be sensitive and listen to their child's reactions.

5. Name and phone number of contact person who can help with the referral process to appropriate agencies to help the student and parents.

6. Name of the person at the school or district the parents can contact about questions and concerns.

7. If meetings for parents have been set up, include the date, time, and place.

All of the precautions and actions that schools must take may seem to be overwhelming but they are absolutely necessary to cover all of the situations that may potentially happen.

9 | Development Programs

Student Development Programs

One of the best resources for curbing violence in schools is the students' awareness of how to deal with everyday life. Schools are busy teaching students the three Rs which are important but many don't teach them the skills they need to deal with everyday problems or the potential of violence and what they can do about it. Parents should be the source of learning some of these skills, but, as was discussed, many parents have never learned or acquired the skills and cannot pass them on. In some cases, the parents have learned or acquired the wrong skills and they pass on skills that will cause their children problems.

The argument can be made that it is not the school's responsibility to teach students skills that are not part of the curriculum and that the curriculum is too full to teach those skills. So the question is, "If schools cannot teach these skills and many parents don't have the skills or have the wrong skills, where will the student get the skills needed to survive?" The answer is, they won't acquire everyday survival skills that will enable them to deal with others.

- ■ Conflict management — Students can be given training in how to deal with conflict situations and this training can start at a very early age. Students in the first or second grade can be given training as to how to deal with a conflict situation and how to resolve it without serious consequences. This training, once started, can be reinforced every year as children progress through school. Many students have no idea how to deal with conflict and what they see in the media and in movies indicates they can handle conflict with aggression.

Students need to learn that conflict is a natural occurrence and if handled properly can be healthy for their development. They also need to learn the constructive and destructive aspects of conflict and what they can do to avoid the destructive aspects. They should understand that dealing with conflict need not be an emotional event where one or more parties is psychologically and emotionally hurt.

Along with conflict management, students can be taught peer mediation and this process can become a part of resolving volatile situations in school. This is a process for resolving disputes and conflict in which a neutral third party acts as a facilitator for the process. In mediation, the object is to work out the differences between the parties in a constructive manner. Mediation can provide schools with an alternative to a traditional disciplinary method or can be used in conjunction with the current disciplinary practices. Students involved in this process learn a new way of handling conflict.

In the mediation process, students are trained to help their classmates identify the problems behind a conflict and to find a suitable solution. Peer mediation is not finding who is right or wrong but how to get along with one another and move beyond the immediate conflict. This process allows each student to tell his story and then lets him know that someone understands his perspective of the situation. However, not all conflicts are suitable for peer mediation. Situations involving assault or other type criminal activities are not referred to a mediation process. Some of the situations that are suitable for peer mediation are:

— Name-calling
— Bullying
— Rumors about students

■ Anger management — Anger is another issue students need to learn to deal with. Students need to learn that it is OK to have angry feelings and what to do about them. They need to learn something about their anger style and how they handle their anger on a daily basis. One of the most important aspects that students need to learn is how long-term anger can affect their lives and that it can be a very destructive.

Students also need to learn to deal with someone who is very angry or is very difficult to deal with. Adults are taught how to deal with difficult people but we forget that students go to school everyday with others who are also difficult to get along with.

■ Stress management — Students need to learn something about stress, what stress is, what it can do to them, and what they can do about it.

Students, just like adults, are being asked to do more and achieve more than ever before.

Students need to learn stress management techniques that will help them deal with the daily frustrations that they have. Some of these daily frustrations can build to large frustrations over a long period of time and cause a student to do something irrational.

■ Assertion skills — These are verbal and nonverbal behaviors that will enable students to maintain the respect they need but at the same time not dominate, manipulate, or abuse other students.

Teacher Development Programs

Along with student development programs, teacher development programs must be implemented. There are skills that teachers do not learn in college and they need these skills to be more effective in the classroom:

■ Listening skills — Teachers and most other people do not listen well. They are good at imparting information to students but many times when students have problems, teachers don't listen. Active listening is not difficult to learn but is sometimes difficult to put into practice.

■ Conflict management skills — Both teachers and students need to know how to effectively deal with conflict. The knowledge of the different conflict strategies and when to use them will empower teachers and help them form a closer relationship with students.

■ Effective disciplining — In many colleges and universities, future teachers are taught the latest in teaching skills and how to use them to help students to learn as effectively as possible. Future teachers are not taught how to effectively discipline students to get them to change inappropriate behaviors. It is imperative that teachers know how to use the discipline process because it may reduce the possibility that a particular student might become violent.

■ Handling difficult students — Teachers must know how to intervene and deal positively with dysfunctional behavior in schools that might not call for discipline. With this type of behavior students exhibit excessive frustration or hostility.

■ Addressing student harassment — Students have the capacity to harass other students in many different ways. Teachers must address these problems and ensure that all students are treated fairly. Also, a recent U.S. Supreme Court decision does allow schools to be sued for not dealing with student harassment. In light of this decision, teaching teachers how to deal with sexual harassment and general harassment is imperative.

■ Behaviors of potentially violent students. Each teacher should know the potential danger signals of a potentially violent student and how to handle the student in the classroom.

Parent Programs

Many schools do not offer parent training and are not equipped to do so. However, if inept or authoritarian parents do need help, more than likely they will not get it. It may be difficult to identify these types of parents but schools could make available to all parents training classes that would help them be more effective as parents. It may be possible with this approach that some of these parents would take advantage of the classes. The classes offered should be the same as would be offered to students and/or teachers: conflict management, discipline skills, assertion skills, dealing with dysfunctional behavior, etc.

10 History of Gangs

angs have been a part of urban culture since the 1800s. Probably the first "bad" gangs may have been the pirates who roamed the seas and plundered whatever they could. Gangs are not illegal and if you look at the definition of a gang in *Webster's Dictionary*, "a group of people who associate or work together," many adults are currently involved in groups that could be considered gangs. The California Attorney General's Office defines a gang as:

> *A loose-knit organization of individuals usually between the ages of 14 and 24. The group has a name, is usually territorial, or claims a certain territory as under its exclusive influence, and is involved in criminal acts. Its members associate together, and commit crimes against other youth gangs or against the general population for property, money, or anything of value.*

The earliest identifiable gangs in the U.S. were formed after the Revolutionary War, which ended in 1783. Some of these gangs were known as Smith's fly gang, the Bowery Boys, the Broadway Boys, and the Fly Boys. Most members of these gangs were in their early teens and 20s and some came from the lower economic classes.

Criminal gangs were first formed in the 1800s because of the growing population and worsening economic problems. Irish immigrants formed the first criminal gangs in New York City. They had dress codes and called their members by code nicknames, much like gangs today. The first Irish gang to have a specific leader was the Forty Thieves organized by Edward Coleman in 1826. The decade before the Civil War was a real heyday for most New York street gangs because of the corruption of city government. Gang membership grew and gangs operated without fear of police interference.

After the Civil War, Jewish, Italian, African-American, and Irish gangs were present in New York. As the immigrant population grew, so did gang membership. In the mid-1800s, Chinese gangs appeared in California. Also, after the civil war, the Ku Klux Klan (KKK) was formed as an all-white group.

In the early 1900s, the U.S. economy worsened and the population grew at a rapid pace. The gap between rich and poor was widening and gangs started to appear all over the county where poor people lived. By the mid-1920s, in Chicago alone there were over 1,300 gangs with a membership of over 25,000. During this time, gang warfare was widespread and fighting took place among ethnic, cultural, and racial lines. In the 1920s and 1930s, the Chicano (Mexican-American) gangs started to rise in Los Angeles.

After World War II, gang membership became younger, the membership became largely nonwhite, drugs were more dominant, firearms were used more frequently, the structure of the gang became more rigid, and society became concerned with gangs. In the 1950s, gang fighting rose to an all time high in cities like New York, Philadelphia, Chicago, Los Angeles, and Detroit. These gang members were usually in their teens. The gang members had a code of dress and used mannerisms to identify one another. In the 1950s, some of the terminology for fighting was "bopping, rumbling, or jitterbugging." Gang members used guns, knives, and homemade weapons such as "zip" guns.

In the 1960s gang violence declined mainly because of the rise in drugs. Where there was a lot of drug use, there was less violence. In the 1970s, gangs were back in full force. Gang membership once again grew and so did the potential for violence. New gangs have emerged along ethnic lines such as Korean and Vietnamese gangs. Gang members had access to semiautomatic weapons. Violence has also changed from the original rumbles. Gangs now fight like guerrillas with sniping from rooftops and drive-by shootings that usually kill innocent people.

Although gangs are more prevalent in larger cities like New York, Los Angeles, and Chicago, gang activities occur in midsized cities like Indianapolis and Fort Wayne, IN, Albuquerque, NM, Little Rock, AR, and Louisville, KY.

There are three types of gangs:

- The Social Gang — A relatively permanent group of individuals who will hang out in a specific location. The members of this type of gang will develop a sense of comradeship and they will often engage in group activities. The members of this gang will usually be the most stable young people in a neighborhood.
- The Delinquent Gang — This is a cohesive group of individuals organized around the principle of monetary gains from delinquent activities. The members will depend on one another to carry out the planned activities. The leader of this type of gang is usually the most competent at stealing and can be an excellent organizer and planner.

Most members are emotionally stable and organize their time around illegal activities.

- The Violent Gang — This type of gang is organized for the members to obtain emotional gratification that violent activities can bring. The members spend a lot of time building arsenals and then planning and carrying out violent acts. The leader of this type of gang tends to be emotionally unstable and he or she has a desire to control others. The leaders and the followers of this type of gang will overestimate the size and the power of their small group. The structure of this type of gang is constantly changing and an ally on one day may be an enemy the next day. One way of identifying this type of gang is by the violence within the group.

In the 1980s and 1990s, gangs took on a different character and moved into many areas that heretofore were unimagined and many of those areas are illegal. Gangs are now spreading from the inner cities to the suburbs. In fact, gang activity for the most part has stabilized in urban areas, but has become an increasing problem in the suburbs.

Street gangs thrive on intimidation, notoriety and often find violence glamorous as well as necessary to maintain their gang status. A street gang depends on both the cooperation of the group and the individual for success. The leader of the gang is often the toughest, has the guns or the most money. The status of leadership is often short-lived. Gang activities usually have the potential for violence and gang members often seek confrontations with rivals which results in violence.

Why Gangs Develop

Gangs are like most organizations. They respond to the needs of their members that are not met through other resources. They provide the member with a sense of family and acceptance that could be lacking in their lives. Gang members often come from homes where they feel alienated from their families, neglected by them or they don't have positive role models in their lives. They may turn to the gang when their needs for love are not being met at home. In some cases, it may be a family tradition to belong to a gang.

Gangs help maintain a strong sense of ethnic identity and ease the problems of racisim. When young people encounter both personal and institutional racism, risks of gangs increase. When groups of young people are denied access to power, privileges, or resources, they will form their own anti-establishment group. The gang gives them a sense of power (something they may never have experienced) and gang activities give them an outlet for the anger caused by racism.

The sense of hopelessness generated by poverty can result in young people not being able to obtain the goods and/or services they need and want. They may find it difficult to meet their basic physical and psychological needs which can affect their self worth and pride. One way to obtain money is to join a gang and get involved in the drug trade.

Many young people are especially susceptible to influence by their peers. They want to be valued by people their own age and they try to seek the company of other young people who will appreciate them. Even young people who are very aggressive will find friends in other young people who do the same thing. This enables them to support one another. Also, fear of another gang and a need for protection at school or in the neighborhood may cause some youths to join a gang.

The media also influences the development of young people. Before many young people have established their own value systems and are able to make rational moral judgments, the media gives them a distorted view of life by promoting drugs, sex, and violence as an acceptable lifestyle. This influence can help young people decide that it is OK to belong to a group that uses all of these as a lifestyle. The *internet* also has an influence in that many of the gangs have internet sites.

Obtaining Membership in the Gang

Most gangs have started accepting members from all racial and ethnic backgrounds and from all socioeconomic backgrounds. Recruits of gangs must usually be "jumped in." This means that they will be required to accept a beating by other gang members or they will be required to commit a crime of some sort. After being jumped in, members are often required to be tattooed to show their loyalty to the gang.

The Gang's Influence

A gang's influence runs much further than providing young people with a sense of security, status and personal value. The gang establishes rules of conduct that define how each member should act under certain circumstances. The young person realizes that by adhering to these standards he will win acceptance to the gang and if he does not adhere to the standards, he will be rejected by the gang.

The young person pays a high price for gang membership. There are the physical risks and dangers from the violent activities that gangs engage in. Most gang members will discard their formal education for the gang and the gang will shape the future of the member, usually with some type of criminal record.

11 Characteristics of Gangs

Most gangs share certain characteristics. Many of them are developed on racial and ethnic lines and for the most part are male (although there is significant growth in female gangs and diversity in male gangs because of multiethnic neighborhoods).

There is strong adherence to the code of the gang that is usually very strict. There tends to be a very strong cohesiveness among gang members that increases as their recognition from society increases. Loyalty and cohesiveness are solidified by the gang member's participation in antisocial and illegal activities. The chain of command of the gang is hierarchical and strictly followed. In present-day gangs, active members are becoming younger and the use of weapons has become much more sophisticated. Members seem to have a total disregard for human life as evidenced by many of the senseless killings and the increase in the numbers of innocent victims.

White Hate Gangs

In the early 1990s, a new crime classification known as "hate crimes" arose. White supremacist gangs such as the Skinheads were largely responsible for committing many of the hate crimes. White hate gangs have existed in the U.S. for many years. The Skinheads originated in England in the 1960s. They originally had long hair, but in the 1970s members began to shave their heads to be unique. They wore boots and suspenders and fought frequently with other groups. The Skinhead movement came across the Atlantic to the U.S. in the mid-1980s and in 1993, there were reportedly 3,500 members across 40 states and the numbers are growing.

The Skinheads are the most violent of all white supremacy groups and have no central Skinhead organization. Many groups that operate independently around the country include the:

- American Front
- Northern Hammerskins
- Aryan Resistance League
- SS of America

The Skinheads are divided into two separate ideologies. The majority of Skinheads are racist, neo-Nazi whites who feel threatened by nonwhites. Another faction, Skinheads Against Racial Prejudice (SHARP), are not racist and will actually fight the other group. Other names for this faction of the Skinheads are:

- Racial Unity Skinheads
- Anti-Racist Action
- Two-Tone Skins
- Mad Skins

Nonwhites can be SHARP members.

Other white supremacist gangs can also be found operating in the U.S. such as:

- Supreme White Power (SWP)
- Aryan Youth Movement (AYM)

A Skinhead is usually between the ages of 13 and 25 and can be male or female. Most of the males shave their heads and do not have facial hair except for sideburns. However, some Skinheads may not have their heads shaved so as to not to draw attention.

A Skinhead usually wears Doctor Martens boots (also called Doc Martens) imported from Europe. These are authentic boots directly from the European Skinhead movement. If these boots are not available, they will wear substitute work boots that lace up the front. Black is the most popular color. They favor the steel-toed boots that are more effective in a fight. They also use shoelaces as identification with white denoting white power; red laces signify that the wearer is prepared to spill blood; green signifies the Skinhead as a gay basher.

The Skinhead member often wears a U.S. Air Force flight jacket with patches or insignias such as swastikas, KKK, or WAR (White Aryan Resistance) emblems. They wear blue or black jeans or military camouflage, and they may wear suspenders (in England, called "braces"). Skinheads will often tattoo symbols such as the SS (lightning bolts), barbed wire (usually around the biceps), swastikas or iron crosses on their bodies. A female Skinhead will dress about the same as the male but will not shave her head, She will wear her hair in a punk-rock style.

The publicity about American Skinheads has increased in the last several years but their growth in numbers has not been large. Most of the time they are seen as intriguing or fascinating and bizarre in appearance. Skinheads espouse extreme prejudice and can be very violent. As a radical movement, their rhetoric and actions probably please a certain segment of society that agrees with their political and social attitudes.

Even if Skinhead membership remains low, they represent a real threat. Even if a young person ceases to be a member of the Skinheads, it does not mean they have forsaken the intense racial beliefs or hostilities. Just because they no longer shave their heads or wear the Doc Marten boots, and are not readily identifiable, it does not necessarily mean their ideologies have changed.

Crips and Bloods

Black gangs have been around for many years. Members of these gangs can range in age from 12 to the late 20s. Black gangs are known as "sets" and may be quite small or very large. The forerunner of the "super gangs" of today was the Young Boys Incorporated (YBI) of Detroit. Most black gangs of today align themselves with these larger gangs:

- **Crips** — Organized in the late 1960s in the Watts, Willowbrook, and Compton sections of Los Angeles. The primary activities of the gang were extorting or robbing students at local schools. Some of the Crips sets are:

East Coast	P.J. Watts	99 Mafia
Playboy Gangsters	Rollin 60s	Watts Bab Loc
Hoover	Front Street	Eight Tray Gangsters
Underground CRIPs		

■ **Bloods** — Organized in the early 1970s as protection and defense against the Crips. They originated in the Compton suburb of Los Angeles and they were originally organized as the Piru Street Boys. Some of the Blood sets are:

Treetop Pirus	Skottsdale Pirus	Be-Bop Watts
Parch Pirus	Krenshaw Mafia	Rolling Twenties
Swans	Patch Pirus	Kabbage Patch

The Crips and Bloods also have a particular way of dressing as a way of identifying themselves. The British Knights footwear was popular with the Crips because the BK stands for Blood Killer. One of the easiest ways to identify a gang member is by his team jacket such as the Starter jacket. Gangs will often identify or adopt a college or professional sports team because their colors are the same as the gang's. The second most obvious way to identify a gang member is the hat or cap and the way it is worn (gang members will often wear them backwards).

Tattoos are another way to identify a gang member. They are found primarily on the hands, arms, chest, back, or legs. They indicate loyalty to the gang and are extensions of gang graffiti.

Folk Nation and People Nation

The Folk Nation and People Nation are ethnically diverse gangs organized in Chicago in the late 1970s. The Folk Nation grew out of an alliance between the Black Gangster Disciples and the Simon City Royals the two largest black and white gangs in Chicago, and some 20 other area gangs. The People Nation, which represents about 18 street gangs, was formed as a protective counter to this alliance by the Vice Lords and the Latin Kings, the largest Hispanic street gangs in Chicago.

The Folk Nation and People Nation use similar clothing, tattoos, etc., to identify themselves as do the Crips and Bloods. However, the Folk Nation will display everything to the right and the People Nation will display everything to the left. For example, if a gang member is wearing a hat with the bill slanting to the right he is a member of the Folk Nation; if it is to the left, he is a member of the People Nation.

Folk Nation Gangs	**People Nation Gangs**
Ambrose	Bishops
Ashland Vikings	Blackstone Rangers/El Rukn

Black Disciples
Black Gangster Disciples
Insane Satan Disciples
Braziers
Brothers of the Struggle (BOS)
C-Notes
Campbell Boys
Gangster Disciples
Harrison Gents
Imperial Gangsters
Latin Disciples
Latin Eagles
Latin Jivers
Latin Lovers
Latin Saints
Latin Souls
Maniac Disciples
Orchestra Albany
Popes
Satan Disciples
Simon City Royals
Spanish Cobras

Cobra Stones
Cullerton Boys
4 Corner Hustlers
Gaylords
Insane Deuces
Insane Unknown
Jousters
Kents
Kool Gang
Latin Counts
Latin Kings (several factions)
P. R. Stones
Party People
Racine Boys
Ridgeway Lords
Sin City Boys
Spanish Lords
Tokers
United Latin Organization
Vice Lords (several factions)
Villa Lobos
Warlords

Hispanic Gangs

Two of the most prominent features of Hispanic gangs are their devout loyalty to the neighborhood and their single-minded devotion to the gang and its members. Kinship within the gang has a long tradition. It is not uncommon to find second and third generation gang members. Fathers take pride in seeing their sons initiated into the gang just as their fathers did.

Hispanic gang member can be separated into three distinct categories:

- Pee wees — Members between the ages of 9 and 13 who will become the new generation of the gang.
- Hard core — members between ages of 14 and 22 who actively carry out the gang's activities.
- Veteranos — members 23 and up who are considered leaders but may not actively participate in the gang's activities. They are highly respected for their past accomplishments and the fact they have lived past the age of 22.

Like most other gangs, Hispanic gangs will wear the latest in athletic shoes. They usually wear Dickie brand pants either in black or khaki that are over-sized at the waist. They favor Pendleton shirts or white tee shirts that are rolled up to reveal tattoos and those shirts are usually oversized. Oversized clothing is useful for concealing weapons. Tattoos are popular among Hispanic male gang members and may be located anywhere on the body.

Asian Gangs

Since 1971, over 3.5 million Asians have immigrated to the U.S. and have es-tablished themselves in both large and small metropolitan areas. The U.S. has been fertile ground for the creation of gangs. The Southeast Asian gangs are not as well organized as other Asian gangs such as the Chinese. They also tend to follow the tradition along the lines of Hispanic gangs in that family mem-bers, relatives, and neighbors tend to belong to the same gang.

Southeast Asian gangs are usually motivated by money and they will pri-marily burglarize businesses or homes for the money. They usually do not ad-here to any hard and fast rules when it comes to their turf and traveling gangs cross state lines to commit crimes. In many instances, the money they ob-tained is used to buy automatic assault rifles and semiautomatic handguns. Parents of these gang members will not see these weapons at home because they are often kept at other locations.

Asian gang members usually dress according to the current fashion. They also may wear the baggy clothes associated with other gangs. Asian gangs will also use tattoos or burn marks on the body for identification.

Tagger Gangs

Tagger gangs are sometimes called crews, cliques, or posses. Taggers are graf-fiti artists and use the city for their canvas. Tagger gangs are made up of teens who use spray paint, felt pens, or paint brushes. Their artwork can be intri-cate, colorful, and complex. Taggers are proud of their artwork and they will take pictures of it because it usually will not last long.

Taggers usually wear nothing special, except for oversized pants to possi-bly carry paint in. They may also carry book bags or knapsacks for paint.

Female Gangs

Females have always been a part of male gangs because they tended to be girl-friends of gang members. They were used by male counterparts to do the incidental work of the gang. Female gang members might transport drugs for male members because females were rarely searched.

In recent years, females have started to form their own gangs. They are usually offshoots of male gangs and they will back one another up in case of a problem. However, the female gangs do not tend to be as demonstrative as their male counterparts. They are more reserved but they are still dangerous. There has been an increase of female gang violence in recent years and violence between female gang members can be just as deadly as among their male counterparts. Female gang members are usually younger than their male counterparts and sometimes range from 11 to 18 years of age.

Female gang members can easily be recognized because their clothing is usually dark and in varying colors of blue, black or brown and tattoos are common. Hispanic female gang members sometimes wear the same basic clothing of male Hispanics and they will usually wear pants rather than dresses. They may wear bandanas around their heads or use them as belts. They wear their own style of jewelry with the exception of a "chola band," which is a black rubber band that is tied around the middle finger of the left hand and pulled across the top of the hand and around the wrist.

Black female gang members have individual styles different from one another. They may wear ordinary clothes but they may be of a specific color to signify to which gang they claim membership. Asian female gang members may dress in short black leather skirts, black tops, black stockings, and spiked heels. Their identification with their gang is discreet and they may wear certain color shoes, paint their fingernails in a specific color, or wear jewelry that will identify them. Their tattoos are burned or cut into the skin and usually in visible places.

12 Gang Language, Hand Signs, Symbols, and Graffiti

G ang members use their own language to communicate with one another. For example, Crips use the word "cuzz" which is a shortened term for "cousin" or they might use the term "BK" for Blood Killer. Bloods avoid using words that begin with "c" to put down Crips or they may use the term "crabs" to "dis" or disrespect the Crips. Members of the Folk Nation use the motto "All is One" to greet one another. The People Nation members use the motto "All is Well" to greet one another. Appendix D is a glossary of gang terms.

Hand signs may be one singular movement or a series of movements using one or both hands. Gangs have learned to use the American Sign Language (ASL) alphabet and numerals to indicate gang affiliation. When a gang member gives a sign to another member it is called "flagging" or "throwing." Members of the Folk Nation throw their signs from the right and members of the People Nation will throw signs from the left. Gang members will give one another hand signs to declare unity or to determine the affiliation of an unknown gang member.

Gang graffiti is used to advertise to the area that the gang exists. Gang names will appear on walls to let other gangs know that the area is their territory. Graffiti will always contain the name of the gang and of the person who wrote the graffiti. The graffiti is used primarily by Hispanic, black and white gangs although Asian gangs are now starting to use graffiti to advertise their presence. Appendix E contains gang alphabets and samples of gang symbols and hand signs.

Gangs and Sports Teams Clothing

An important indicator of gang involvement is sports team apparel. Gang members use popular professional and college sports clothing to represent individual gangs. However, it should be noted that the sporting clothing does not always signify gang affiliation. The following list is how various gangs use sports clothing:

Team	Gang	How used
Atlanta Braves	People	Initial "A" for Almighty
Boston Celtics	Spanish Cobra	Colors green and black
British Knights	Crip	Initials "BK" for Blood Killers
Burger King	Crip	Initials "BK" for Blood Killers
Charlotte Hornets	Corner Hustlers	Initials "C" and "H"
Charlotte Hornets	Imperial Gangsters	Colors black and pink
Chicago Bulls	Vice Lords	Colors black and red
	Latin Counts	
	Mickey Cobras/ Cobrastones	
Chicago Bulls	Black Peace Stones Nation	"BULLS" stands for "Boy U Look Like Stone"
Chicago Blackhawks	Vice Lords	Colors black and red; Pitch-Fork Star
Chicago Cubs	Spanish Cobras	Initial "C"
Cincinnati Reds	4 Corner Hustlers	Put a "4" next to the "C" and an "H" Inside of the "C"
Colorado Rockies	Simon City Royals	Place a white "S" in front of the "C"
Columbia Knights	Bloods	Initials "CK" for Crip Killer
Converse AllStar Shoes	People	Five-point star in the logo of the label
Dallas Cowboys	People	Five-point star
Denver Broncos	Black Disciples	Switch "DB" for "BD"
Detroit Lions	Gangster Disciples	Colors black and blue
Detroit Tigers	Folks	Initial "D" for Disciples
Detroit Tigers	Gangster Disciples	Colors black and blue
Duke	Folks	Colors Black and Blue; "DUKE"="Disciples Utilizing Knowledge Everyday"
Duke	Folks	Crown going down as disrespect to Kings
Georgetown	Folks	Initial "G" for Gangster
Georgetown Hoyas	Gangster Disciples	Colors black and blue; "HOYAS" stands for "Hoover's On Your Ass"

Georgia Tech	Folks	Initial "G" for Gangster
Kansas City Royals	Folks	Colors black and blue
Kansas City Royals	Simon City Royals	"Royals"
LA Dodgers	Gangster Disciples	Initial "D" for Disciples
LA Kings	Latin Kings	"Kings"
LA Kings	People	"KINGS" stands for "Kill Inglewood Nasty Gangsters"
Louis Vuitton Cap	Vice Lords	Initials "LV" reversed
Miami Hurricanes	People	Color orange
Miami Hurricanes	Future Stones	Color orange
Michigan	MLDs	Initial "M" for Maniac Latin Disciples
Minnesota Twins	MLDs	Initial "M" for Maniac Latin Disciples
NY Yankees	Gangster Disciples	Colors Black, blue, and white
North Carolina Tar Heels	Folks	Colors: Black and blue
Nike	Folks	Colors: Black and blue
Oakland A's	Ambrose	Initial "A" for Ambrose
Oakland A's	Orchestra Albany	Initials "O" and "A"
Oakland A's	Spanish Cobras	Color green
Los Angeles Raiders	Folks	"RAIDERS" stands for "Ruthless Ass Insane Disciples Running Shit"
Los Angeles Raiders	People	"RAIDERS" stands for "Raggedy Ass Iced Donuts Everywhere Running Scared" used to disrespect Folks
Los Angeles Raiders	Gangster Disciples	Colors
Orlando Magic	Folks	"MAGIC" stands for "Maniacs (MLDs) and Gangsters in Chicago"; Colors black and blue represent many "Folks" gangs
Philadelphia Phillies	People	Initial "P" for People
Phoenix Suns	Black Peace Stone	Color; Initials "P" and "S"
Pittsburgh Pirates	People	Initial "P"; Colors black and gold for Latin Kings
Pittsburgh Pirates	Bloods	Initial "P" stands for Piru (Bloods)
San Francisco Giants	Folks	Switch initials for "Super Gangster Folk"
San Francisco Giants	Future Stones	Initials "S" and "F" spelled backwards
San Francisco (any)	Stone Freaks	Initials "S" and "F"
St Louis Cardinals	Spanish Vice Lords	Basic red hat

Team	Gang	How used
Starter Symbol	Folks	Crack the five-point star to disrespect the People gang
Starter Symbol	People	Five-point star
Tampa Bay Lightning	Gangster Disciples	Color black and blue
Texas Rangers	People	Initial "T" looks like pitchfork going down
University of Illinois	Folks	Initials "U" and "I" together appear to be a pitchfork going down
University of Indiana	Imperial Gangsters and Folks	Initials "U" and "I" overlapping appear to make the shape of a pitchfork showing Folks affiliation
UNLV	Vice Lords	Colors red and black; UNLV backwards stands for "Vice Lords Nation United"

13 Gangs and Schools

Historically, schools have been neutral territory, especially suburban schools, but they are now used to recruit new gang members and serve as a place where young gang members can get together. Gangs can easily spread from school to school as student gang members transfer from a school with gangs to a school without gangs.

Few young people actually join gangs. That does not mean the school they attend will not suffer some sort of gang-related violence. Gangs are many times involved in the trafficking of drugs and weapons and the fact that they are present in a school can increase the tensions for everyone in the school. Even though the gang may not be the impetus of the violence, students may arm themselves for protection from gangs and this could indirectly cause some form of violence. Many gang members stay in school so they can congregate and discuss gang activities, display the strength of their membership, provide protection for members, and engage in illegal or violent activities.

Law enforcement agencies maintain gang data and release it to the public. School administrators may not be as quick to acknowledge the existence of gangs in schools and this makes it difficult to get accurate data on gang activity. Students are not as reluctant as administrators to deny the existence of gangs.

Some Signs of Gangs in Schools

Each school district is reflective of the community in which it resides. Many schools and school districts have already seen the need for internal security and gang squads to help curb the growth of gangs in schools. This may be second nature to larger cities where gangs and gang violence may already be common. For some smaller cities and suburban schools gangs may be something new that they need to learn about. However, each school district must keep close watch on the gang activity in its schools no matter what size or where they are located. Some of the potential indicators of gangs in schools are:

- Graffiti — The first appearance of graffiti may be in the washrooms and other areas that are seldom monitored and move to other areas as the gang members become more secure.
- Clothing — Although all styles of dress do not indicate gang problems the appearance of clothes that have been altered may be an indication of a problem.
- Increase of crime and vandalism — Vandalism in the school and the surrounding community may be an indicator that something is the wrong. The commission of crimes such as damage to property, assault, burglary, auto theft, and rape may be necessary for admittance to the gang.
- Weapons on school campus — More weapons on campus may indicate gang activity. Some students may be carrying weapons for protection from gang members.
- Decline in attendance — This may signal potential for gang violence and students might not go to school to avoid gangs, especially during gang recruitment time.
- Tattoos — Students who did not have tattoos, who then get them, may be indicating their gang allegiance.
- Use of vocabulary and hand signs — Often when there is gang activity, students will start to use a new vocabulary or start flashing hand signs. Sometimes the use of these is very subtle and must be looked for very closely.

One thing to remember is that the absence of definite signs of gang activity does not mean that there is none. It might be really easy to think that everything is under control if no signs are present but this might only lull a school into a false sense of security.

14 Gang Management in Schools

We have established that gangs have a significant impact on violence and crime in schools in a different way than the mass killer. Responding to gangs and gang activity can take a great deal of an administrator's time and energy. However, schools are not powerless to respond. Many times though, schools, because they feel powerless or because gangs are omnipotent factors, react in a harsh manner or they don't react at all.

Schools need to plan a strategy that mobilizes both school and community resources to offer viable alternatives to gang membership. To be successful, the strategy must be built on the sociopsychological reasons why gangs develop and attract young people. The schools and community must find a way to address the lack of self esteem and powerlessness many students have. The strategy must include an understanding of the gang psychology that enables gangs to attract new members and retain existing members.

The following strategy may help prevent gang membership and potential violent gang activities in schools:

1. Involve parents by offering them:
   - Educational programs on gangs and how to deal with them. The program should be presented in a culturally sensitive way and if necessary in different languages to reflect cultural diversity of the community. Parents need to know why gangs are formed and how gang members recruit new members. They also need to know what signs to look for to determine that their child may be involved in gang activity.
2. As part of the school curriculum:
   - Establish moral and ethical educational standards.

- Include values clarification.
- Include conflict management.
- Include anger management.
- Offer programs to students about gangs, their destructiveness, and how students can avoid being drawn into the gang culture. Doing this in small groups will help allow students to talk more freely about their school experiences and what they hope to gain from them.

3. Create a school atmosphere where students want to come because they feel valued.
   - Create a motivating environment where students are able to believe they can reach their potential.
   - Don't maintain an autocratic atmosphere where the only time students hear anything from teachers and administrators is when they do something wrong. Reward positive behavior the same as you would correct negative behavior.
   - Allow students to have some input into shaping their environments. Students would like to be included in formulating the policies that affect their behavior and their environment. When students have input, they will have more of a desire to see a policy work.
   - Don't overreact to situations that call for no action.

4. Target students who seem to be vulnerable to gang recruitment for special assistance by:
   - Peer counseling.
   - Support groups.
   - Mentoring.
   - Extra training in conflict resolution and anger management strategies.

5. Educate all school and support staff on:
   - The history of gangs.
   - How and why gangs develop.
   - How to spot gang activity in the school.
   - How to respond to gangs and gang activity.

6. Monitor all youths not enrolled in school but "hang out" on or near school grounds.
   - If necessary, increase security personnel monitoring these youths.
   - Identify and pay close attention to known gang leaders or students who have transferred from other schools because of gang activity.

7. Make an assessment, at least twice a year, of the success of your anti-gang program, and make adjustments when necessary.

Dress Codes

Young people communicate their identity through their appearance and their appearance is very complex. Meaning, change, fashion, and context will all interweave into appearance to make the statement the youth wants. With gangs, specific clothing, as indicated, communicates very clear meanings. To reduce the significance of gang appearance in schools, there has been a move by many schools to use dress codes and many of them have been very effective in curtailing gang clothing. Current fashions need to be continually monitored and there should be a ban on apparel that indicates a relationship with a gang. Other items that need to be controlled are:

- Accessories such as jewelry, shoes, or hats
- Tattoos
- Hand signs
- Posture

These things may be more difficult to control but they have as much significance as clothing.

In some instances, parents, school officials, and some government officials have encouraged the use of school uniforms. Rather than developing a dress code, schools are mandating uniforms for all students. These uniforms are thought to eliminate the deliberate or chance wearing of gang clothing. However, even though uniforms are used, they are not necessarily the panacea that will keep students from using clothing as a means of identifying themselves as gang members. The way a student wears a collar on his uniform, a small thread sewed into a uniform or some other variation may still identify a gang member.

Gang Squads

Schools in large cities often have their own security departments. The departments may include a special group that is dedicated specifically to gang and gang control. These groups are for the most part successful in inhibiting gang activity. They also work closely with police department gang specialists in those cities and they do this very effectively. Since gangs are now moving into suburban schools, it may be necessary for these schools to consider the use of this type of group to maintain control over gangs. School security squads should be trained in:

1. The school's rules and policies regarding discipline.
2. Current fads that are popular in the community including:
   - Clothing
   - Hair styles
   - Slang
3. Gang identifiers.
4. How to communicate with students and how to listen for rumors that are circulating within the school.

Conclusion

This is not a book that will solve every major problem with school violence or gangs. We do not believe that violence will totally be eliminated from schools or that gangs will disappear. However, we hope that school violence *does not* become a common phenomenon. School violence will happen again and it is very difficult to predict when or where it will happen.

This book is meant to help schools to develop plans that will deter or even prevent another event like Littleton, CO, from happening again.

Appendix A

"Copycat" Threats

After every major act of school violence "copycat" responses and threats are common. Since perceived or falsely reported situations will often produce the same reactions as a real event, the reactions and needs of students, staff may be identical to the real event. The Crisis Management Team must take the necessary steps to insure that "copycat" responses are investigated and handled in the appropriate manner.

Appendix B

Unsafe Building Evacuation Plan (Fire, Bomb Threat, Etc.)

A drill for this type of situation should be practiced at least three times per school year. All drills should be thoroughly planned and scheduled ahead of time and all school staff should know when the drill will take place. Agencies should be notified that a drill will be taking place and a record kept of the date and time it took place. A follow-up assessment of the drill should be made with the Crisis Management Team to see if any changes should be made. The following procedures will be followed for a drill:

An alarm is sounded or instructions are given to leave a building:

- Teachers of individual classrooms are responsible for taking their class rosters with them and leading the students from the classes out of the building through designated exits to a predesignated area free of overhead power lines, gas lines, traffic and emergency vehicles.
- Students will not take any personal items with them.
- Assigned staff members, not in charge of classrooms, will check all rest rooms, cafeterias, classrooms, etc., for people left behind.
- Teachers will follow an established procedure to assist handicapped students.
- Assigned staff will take emergency equipment to a predesignated area.
- Students will remain calm and orderly.
- Teachers will take attendance to make sure every student is accounted for.

- Any student not accounted for will be reported (by name) to a designated person such as the principal and an immediate search for that student will begin.
- Appropriate agencies will be notified by the designated staff.

If an alarm is sounded that is not preplanned:

- The determination will immediately be made if it is false or real.
- If it is false, an announcement will immediately be made notifying all occupants to stay where they are and not leave the school.
- If it is determined to be real, the appropriate procedures will be followed as in the drills.
- Assigned staff will turn off gas, electricity, etc.
- Use a predetermined method to release students to appropriate adults.
- Take remaining students to an alternate site where they can stay until they are released.

Appendix C

Bomb Threats

Preparation for bomb threats:

- A bomb threat can be received at a school at any time. To provide a safe environment and to reduce the potential for planting a bomb in a school, the following precautions should be taken:
  - All rooms not in use should be kept locked
  - All storage areas and miscellaneous areas should be kept locked at all times
  - Staff should be trained to observe anything out of the ordinary in the school
  - The school must be secured during the times it is not in use
  - Train staff what to do if a bomb threat is called in or mailed to the school
  - Train staff on the psychological profile of a bomb threat caller
  - Train staff on the general appearance of homemade bombs
  - Train staff to ask these questions of caller:
    - When will it go off?
    - What kind of bomb is it?
    - Where are you now?
- If a bomb threat is received:
  - Remain calm
  - Listen to the caller and do not interrupt him or her
  - Try to write the entire message as it is given

— Try to signal another staff member to notify the principal
— After the caller has hung up, fill out the Bomb Threat Form
— Evacuate the building
— Notify the appropriate local law enforcement agency
— Notify school security

Bomb Threat Form

Date:_____

Time:_____

Caller is:

    Male: ____   Female: ____   Adult: ____   Juvenile: ____

Origin of call:

    Local: ____   Long distance: ____   Inside: ____   Outside: ____

Caller's voice characteristics:

    Loud: ____   Deep: ____   Excited: ____

Caller's language:

    Excellent: ____   Poor: ____

Caller's accent:

    Local: ____   Foreign: ____   Could not identify: ____

Caller's manner:

    Rational: ____   Angry: ____   Coherent: ____   Emotional: ____

Background noise:

    Music: ____   Factory: ____   Animal: ____   Planes: ____   Mixed: ____

Any other features about the call or caller: _____

Appendix D

A Glossary of Terms

Gangs are no different from other subgroups in our society in that they have a special language that they use as a common bond and a barrier to people outside of the gang. This language is constantly evolving and changing across regions and with the different subgroups.

Gang Terminology

AA:	Aid and assist
Ace Cool/Ace Kool:	Best friend/partner
Above board:	Honest and truthful
All is one:	Motto of unity used by members of the Folk Nation
All is well:	Motto of unity used by members of the People Nation
Baile:	To fight (used by Hispanic gangs)
Baller:	A big drug dealer (used by Bloods)
Bangin:	Gang-banging or being in a gang
Bank:	Lots of money
Barrio:	Neighborhood (used by Hispanic gangs)
Base head:	Cocaine smoker
Beatdowns:	Physical assaults
Belittle yourself:	False flagging (giving false hand signs and misrepresenting Affiliation)
BG:	Baby gangster
Big boy:	A higher-up gang member

Bit:	Time in jail
BKA:	Blood Killer Always
Blade:	Knife
Blob:	Derogatory name for Bloods (used by Crips)
Blood:	A fellow gang member
Blowman:	A gang member chose to use a gun
Bo(w):	Marijuana
Boned out:	Quit, chicken out
Book:	To run away or leave
Booyah:	Sound of a shotgun
Braces:	British term for suspenders
Brand:	Tattoo
Breakdown:	Shotgun
Bucket:	Older beat-up car
Bullet:	One-year jail term
Bumping titties:	Fighting
Burn:	Steal or cheat
Burner:	A gang member known for shooting
Bust a cap:	Shoot at an opposing gang member
Bustin a nut:	Having sex with a female
Bussin':	Shoot at an opposing gang member
Busted:	Arrested or shoot at someone
Buster:	A person that wants to be a gangster
Busting:	Involved in a fight using fist or weapons
Buzzed:	Being high or drunk
Caca:	Drugs
Can you dig it?:	Do you understand?
Cap:	Shoot
Catch a cold:	To get killed
Chante:	Residence (used by Hispanic gangs)
Chavala:	Girlfriend (used by Hispanic gangs)
Check it out:	Listen to what I have to say
Chill out:	Take it easy
Chipping:	Occasional use of narcotics
Cholo:	Crazy life (used by Hispanic gangs)
Chota:	Police (used by Hispanic gangs)
Chuco:	Veteran Hispanic gang member
CK:	Crip Killer
Claim:	To announce your gang affiliation

Clocking dollars:	Making money
Cluck:	Cocaine smoker
Colors:	Gang colors
Colom:	Colombian marijuana
Courting in:	Initiating someone into the gang
Courting out:	Expelling someone from the gang
Crab:	Derogatory name for Crips (used by Bloods)
Crank:	Speed
Cripping:	Gang banging (used by Crips)
Crossover:	To go to another gang
Curb serving:	Selling crack on a street corner
Cuzz:	A name Crips call one another
D:	Drugs
Dancing:	Fighting
Dead president:	Money
Dead rag:	A red handkerchief (used by bloods)
Deep:	Heavy conversation
Demonstration:	Fight between gangs
Deuce and a quarter:	Buick Electra 225
Dis, Dissin:	Put down or act disrespectful
Do a ghost:	Leave the scene
Donut:	Derogatory name for Disciples (used by Vice Lords)
Draped:	Wearing a lot of gold jewelry
Drop a dime:	Snitch
Drive-by:	Shooting from a moving vehicle
Dusted:	Under the influence of PCP
Enforcer:	Gang member who dispenses discipline
Essay:	A Hispanic gang member
Faded:	Show disrespect
False flagging:	Showing false gang affiliation
Federated:	Term used by Crips to show disrespect for the color red (Bloods' color)
Fell down:	Stabbed
Five High-Six Die:	Vice Lord term to show contempt for the Disciples
Fire up:	Shoot someone
Flakes:	Derogatory name for Latin Kings
Flashing:	Displaying gang hand signs

Flying your colors:	Representing your gang colors
Four-five:	Forty-five caliber gun
From the shoulders:	To fight
Futures:	Young gang members
Gauge:	Shotgun
Geek:	Someone who is high
Get down:	To fight
Get off my case:	Leave me alone
Getting waxed:	Having sex with a female
Ghetto star:	Gang leader
Girl:	Homosexual
Good monks:	Good people
Go off:	Act crazy
Grease:	To kill someone
G-ride:	Stolen car
Gunned up:	Having an arsenal of guns
Hard:	Tough
Hard look:	Hard stare
Ho:	Whore
Homeboy, Homey:	Male friend, associate gang member
Homegirl:	Female friend, associate gang member
Homey:	Someone from the neighborhood
Hook:	Imitation, punk
Hoo-rah:	Talking loud
Hustler:	Individual "street" money maker
Illing:	Not thinking clearly
Inca:	Gang president (used by hispanic gangs)
Ink:	Tattoo
In the mix:	Busy involved in gang activity
Jack move:	To commit a holdup
Jacked up:	Beat up, assaulted
Jiving:	Lying, attempting to fool someone
Juice:	Influence or power
Jumped in:	Initiated into gang
Jumped out:	Leave the gang
Junior:	Young gang member
Jura:	Police (used by hispanic gangs)
Kibbles and bits:	Small pieces of crack cocaine
Kicking back/kicking it	Taking it easy
Kick you down:	To set up in the middle of a drug transaction

Kicking your hat:	Tilting the hat in a certain way
Kool:	OK
Lady:	Girlfriend
Let's bail:	Let's leave
Lifts:	Vehicle hydraulic shocks
Lit up:	Shot
Loc:	Loco, crazy (used by Hispanic gangs)
Lok:	Loco
Manifesto:	Written rules/gang history
Main man:	Best friend/backup
Making bank:	Making money
Man:	Law enforcement officials
Mark:	Want-to-be gang member
Married:	Joined a gang
Midget:	Young gang member
Mission:	Drive-by shooting/hit
Mobbing:	Hanging out
Molded/scratch:	Embarrassed
Mud duck:	Ugly female
Mud people:	Derogatory name for African-Americans (used by Skinheads)
Nation:	Gang as a whole
Neutron:	Not a gang member
Nut up:	To be mad
O/G:	Original gangster
Off brands:	Rival gangs
Oi:	Skinhead greeting/music
On line:	Proper behavior
On the pipe:	Free-basing cocaine
On the up and up:	The facts
One time:	Police
Outs:	Out of prison
Packing:	Carrying a gun
Pay the bills:	Stab a person
Playboy:	Ladies' man
Pee wee:	Young gang member
People:	Vice Lords and affiliates
Phildoras:	Not expensive (used by Hispanic gangs)
Pica:	Cocaine (used by Hispanic gangs)
Pimped out:	Well-dressed

Pintada:	Gang graffiti (used by Hispanic gangs)
Piru:	Another name for a Blood
Poo butt:	Sissy
Posse:	Gang
Primo:	Good drugs
Puffer:	Cocaine smoker
Pugging:	Fighting
Punk:	Homosexual
Put'em in check:	Discipline someone
Put in some work:	Do a shooting
Putting you on:	Making a fool of you
Puto:	Homosexual (used by Hispanic gangs)
Rag:	Color of gang handkerchief
Raise:	Leave
Ran up on:	Robbed
Rap:	To talk, type of music
Rap sheet:	Criminal record
Raspberry:	Female who takes anything for sex or drugs
Rat packin':	Ganging up on someone
Recruiting:	Looking for girls
Rep:	Reputation
Represent:	Show gang affiliation
Ride:	Automobile
Ride on:	Go to a rival gang neighborhood
Righteous:	Upstanding
R.I.H.:	Rest in hell (used in graffiti)
R.I.P.:	Rest in peace (used in graffiti/remembrance of a fallen gang member)
Rock:	Crack cocaine
Road dog:	Best friend
Rod:	Gun
Roll:	Rob someone, or a cigarette
Ru (rooster):	Piru
Saggin':	Wearing pants low around the waist
Scag:	Heroin
School them:	Instruct younger gang members
Scratch:	Money
Shank:	Knife
Shooter:	Gang member who uses firearms
Six Alive-Five Die:	Term used to insult the People Nation

Six Pop-Five Drop:	Term used to insult the People Nation
Skeezer:	Ugly female
Slangin':	Selling drugs
Slipping in the dark:	Getting stabbed
Slow your roll:	Take it easy
Smoke 'em:	Kill them
Snaps:	Money
Snow bunny:	White female
Soft:	Weak
Stacking:	Throwing another gang's sign upside down to show disrespect of that gang
Step to me:	Challenge
Straight:	Things are all right
Straight up:	Honest
Sucker crews:	Rival gangs
Sup?:	What's up?
Tag:	Graffiti signature
Talking head:	Arguing/wanting to fight
Tall:	Large in numbers
Throw a switch:	Misrepresent gang affiliation
Throw down the crown:	Term used to insult Latin Kings
Tight:	Close to someone
Tonto:	Stupid person
TOS:	Order of execution, Terminate On Sight
Three eight:	.38-caliber handgun
Trick on someone:	Inform on someone
Turf:	Area held by specific gang
V-Code:	Gang regulations
Vato:	Dude (used by Hispanic gangs)
Veteranos:	Older gang members (used by Hispanic gangs)
Vicky Lous:	Derogatory name for Vice Lords
Violation:	Breaking a gang rule
Wack:	Kill someone
Wacked:	Killed by someone
Wanna-be:	Person who wants to be a gang member
What it B like?:	Blood greeting
What it C like?:	Crip greeting
What up, G?:	Gangster greeting
Wilding:	Gang assault
Zapped:	Killed

Drug Terminology

Amped out:	Fatigued from being under the influence of methamphetamine
Angel dust:	Crystal form of PCP
Base head:	Individual hooked on cocaine
Beam me up:	Looking for drugs
Bird:	Kilo of cocaine
Blow:	Cocaine
Bogey:	Piece of crack cocaine worth $100
Brown paint:	Term used for heroin
C:	Cocaine
Coke spoon:	Small spoon used for inhaling cocaine
Crackhead:	Crack cocaine user
Crank:	Methamphetamine
Crash:	Come down from being high on drugs
Crystal:	Methamphetamine
Do up:	Inject drugs
Dropper:	Syringe
Dusted:	Under the influence of crack cocaine or PCP
Eight ball:	One-eighth ounce of cocaine
8-track:	Two and one half ounces of cocaine
Fix:	Inject a drug
Flash:	The euphoria that follows taking a drug
Flip crip:	A drug house that sells small amounts of drugs
Freak:	A heavy drug user
Fried:	Brain damage due to heavy drug use
Girl:	Cocaine
Graveyard:	A closed drug house
Head:	Drug user
High roller:	Drug dealer
Hubba:	Crack cocaine
Ice:	Crystal methamphetamine
Kit:	Drug injection paraphernalia
Lab:	A place to manufacture narcotics
Love:	Crack cocaine
OZ:	An ounce of drugs
Point:	A needle
Primo:	Marijuana laced with cocaine
Rock:	Piece of crack cocaine
Rollin' good:	Selling drugs

Safe houses:	A place where there is a large amount of drugs and money stored
Stingin' keys:	Selling drugs
Snort:	Sniffing a drug through the nose
Snow:	Cocaine
Speed:	Methamphetamine
Spun:	Overdosed on methamphetamines
Speedball:	A mix of heroin and some type of stimulant
Tie off:	A tourniquet used to inject drugs
Uncut:	A pure form of a drug
Wired:	Under the influence of a drug

Weapon Terminology

AK:	AK-47 automatic, 7.62-caliber assault rifle
Uzi:	9-mm automatic machine pistol
Mac 10/11:	Two 9-mm machine pistols of small size
9-mm:	Standard European pistol caliber
.38/tray eight:	.38-caliber pistol
.22/deuce:	.22-caliber pistol
.44:	.44-caliber pistol
M-16:	U.S. Military rifle
AR-15:	U.S. Military rifle
Car-15:	U.S. Military rifle
Saturday night special:	Cheap pistol, easily available
Automatic:	A weapon that will produce multiple shots when the trigger is pulled
Semiautomatic:	A weapon that fires a single shot each time the trigger is pulled
Bust a cap:	Shoot at someone
Packing:	Carrying a weapon
Assault rifle:	Weapon that can fire in automatic or semiautomatic mode
Magazine:	A spring-loaded box in a pistol's handle that holds ammunition
Revolver:	Pistol that has ammunition in a cylinder above the trigger mechanism
Shotgun:	Weapon that is single- or double-barreled and size is measured in gauge. The barrel can be shortened for concealment, known as a "sawed-off" shotgun.
Dumdum:	Type of bullet designed to be very lethal

Appendix E

The following pages contain the alphabets used by some gangs as well as a sample of gang symbols and hand signs.

ALPHABETS

	CRIPS	GANG-STERS	KINGS	VICE LORDS
A				
B				
C				
D				
E				
F				
G				
H				
I				
J				
K				
L				
M				

	CRIPS	GANG-STERS	KINGS	VICE LORDS
N				
O				
P				
Q				
R				
S				
T				
U				
V				
W				
X				
Y				
Z				

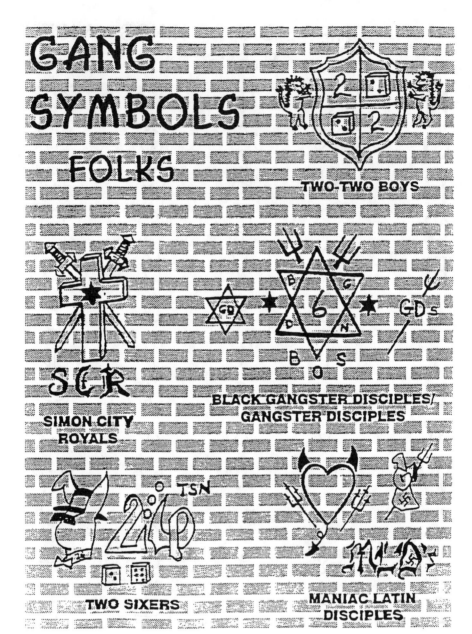

GANG SYMBOLS

FOLKS

TWO-TWO BOYS

SIMON CITY ROYALS

BLACK GANGSTER DISCIPLES/ GANGSTER DISCIPLES

GDs

TWO SIXERS

MANIAC LATIN DISCIPLES

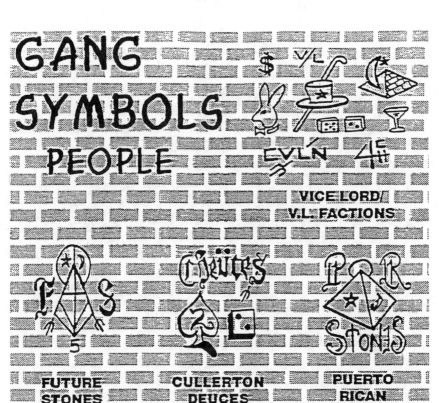

GANG SYMBOLS
PEOPLE

VICE LORD/
V.L. FACTIONS

FUTURE
STONES

CULLERTON
DEUCES

PUERTO
RICAN
STONES

LATIN KINGS

MICKEY COBRAS

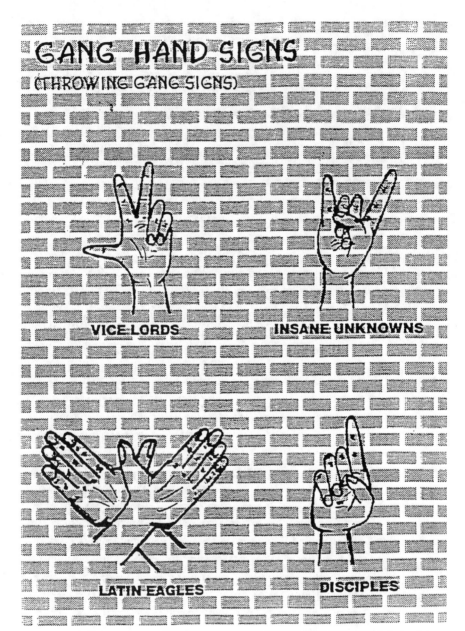

GANG HAND SIGNS
(THROWING GANG SIGNS)

VICE LORDS

INSANE UNKNOWNS

LATIN EAGLES

DISCIPLES

GANG HAND SIGNS
(THROWING GANG SIGNS)

MANIAC LATIN DISCIPLES

SPANISH COBRAS

TWO-SIX BOYS

DISCIPLES & FOLKS

GANG HAND SIGNS
(THROWING GANG SIGNS)

LATIN COUNTS   **DEUCES**

LATIN KINGS   **FUTURE STONES**

GANG HAND SIGNS
(THROWING GANG SIGNS)

BLACK GANGSTER DISCIPLES

IMPERIAL GANGSTERS

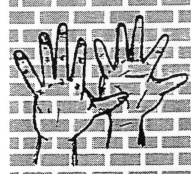

VICE LORDS

SIMON CITY ROYALS

Appendix F

This appendix illustrates gang migration in the U.S. from 1987 through 1992. These three pages indicate how rapidly gang proliferation spread in that time period. As indicated by the increase of gang activities in schools, there has undoubtedly been more proliferation of gangs throughout U.S. since 1992. Also, gang growth has been helped due to use by gangs of new methods of recruitment such as the internet.

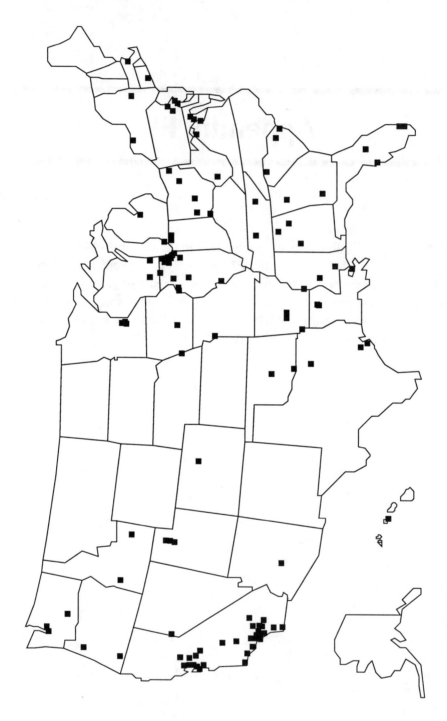

Gang member migration through 1987

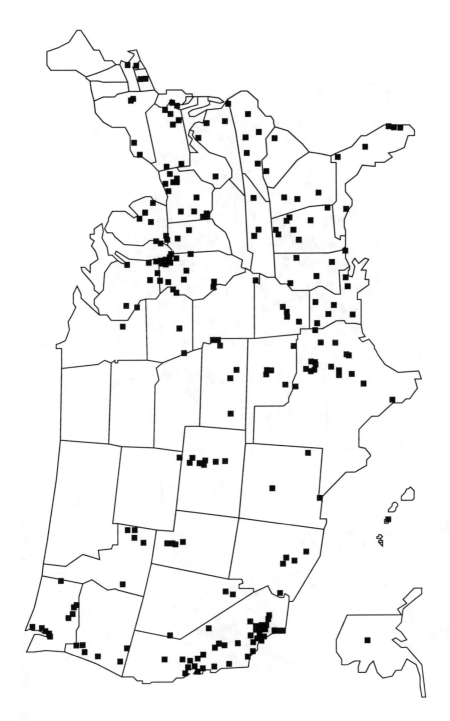

Gang member migration through 1989

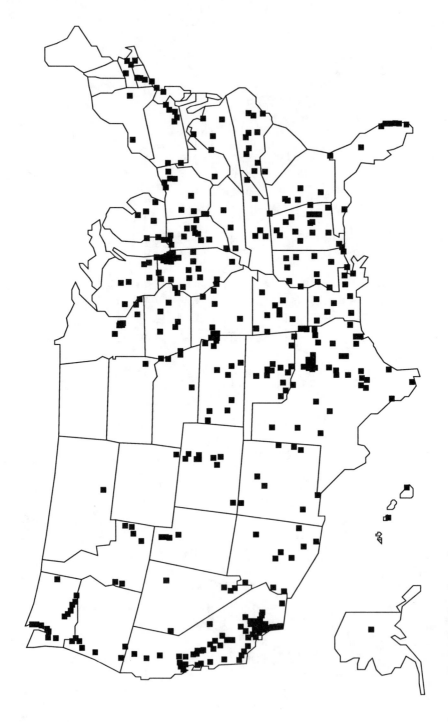

Gang member migration through 1992

Appendix G

Comforting an Injured Student

B eing injured is a frightening experience for anyone, but being injured in a school shooting can be especially frightening for young people. If you are a caregiver for children or teenagers injured in a shooting, it is important to stay calm and reassuring in order to ease their fears and gain their confidence that you can help them. It is important to think of yourself as the students' mirror because they will react to what they see in your face. If they see panic and your overreacting, they will do the same. You need to set the example by staying relaxed and confident so they will calm down and listen to you.

When giving first aid:

- Take a breath and relax.
- Take charge by asking for cooperation from other students and teachers and, if necessary, send someone to get help.
- Stay with the injured student while waiting for qualified help to arrive. You will be a comfort to him or her.
- Tell the student, in a calm manner, that everything will be all right and that help is on the way.
- If you have knowledge of first aid, you may give as much aid as you can, such as treat for shock by:
  — Maintaining an open airway.
  — Elevating the feet (except for head injury).
  — Maintaining a normal body temperature.

Appendix H

Conflict Management Course Outline

1. Perception
   - Why perception is important in everyday life
   - How it affects what we think and what we do
2. Communications basics:
   - How we communicate
     — Orally
     — Written
     — Nonverbally
     — Listening
   - Barriers to effective communication
   - Meaning of non-verbal communications
   - Diversity in communication
   - Active (effective) listening
3. Definition of conflict:
   - It should be emphasized that conflict is a natural occurrence and can be healthy if handled properly
4. Constructive aspects of conflict:
   - It builds cohesiveness among people and groups
   - It opens up discussion of issues that are unresolved
   - It helps an individual grow and learn to deal with future conflicts
   - It can result in the resolution of a problem
5. Destructive aspects of conflict:
   - It may destroy the morale of an individual or group
   - It may divide people and polarize them

- It may produce irresponsible behavior
- If no solution is reached, the problem remains

6. Sources of conflict, such as:
   - Personality clashes
   - Different values, attitudes, needs, or expectations
   - A threat to an individual's status
   - Contrasting perceptions
7. Methods of conflict management:
   - Avoidance
   - Win/lose
   - Accommodation
   - Compromise
   - Collaboration
8. Steps for resolving conflict:
   - Explore the causes of the conflict
     — Making sure the parties have the correct perception of the conflict
     — Remaining open and objective to the causes
   - Getting the best assessment of the situation possible by asking these questions:
     — Have we misinterpreted each other's goals?
     — Is there a personality clash?
     — Does each person have different values?
     — Do we really want to resolve the conflict?
   - Developing alternative solutions to the conflict
     — Assume there is a solution to the conflict because an imperfect solution may be better than no solution at all
     — Focus on the interests of the parties
     — Be sure to give consideration to all of the alternative solutions
   - Agreeing on a solution with these things in mind:
     — Is everyone speaking the same language?
     — Agree on the responsibilities of each party
   - Implement the solution
   - Evaluate the solution
     — Did the solution work? Why/why not?
   - Use a third party mediator if necessary

When planning a conflict resolution class it should be remembered that students will learn better if they are given a chance to practice the skills they learn. Role-playing should be an integral part of the class and this will give the students a chance to practice even though it is not a real situation.

Peer Mediation Outline

Peer mediation may arise from a number of different situations. Students may become emotionally involved in a conflict and may not use rational thought processes. A third party or peer may do more that just implement the conflict resolution process. A peer may:

- Help in reducing tension in the situation
- Help to reduce the possibility of violence
- Control the number of issues that the students are trying to resolve
- Enhance the communications between the students
- Help establish a common ground between the students

The task of the peer mediator is to work face-to-face with the students and it should be done carefully. A student designated to be a peer mediator should be acceptable to all of the students involved in a conflict and one who is not close friends with one of the students. The mediator must be a *neutral* third party. The mediation process must be perceived to be fair to all students involved. Not all students who want to be peer mediators will be capable. In order to train peer mediators, they should attend the conflict class and then do additional work in dealing with conflict as a third party. They should have skills in:

- Perception
- Communication, specifically listening skills
- Conflict resolution
- Questioning skills
- Problem assessment

They should have knowledge of the mediation process:

- Initial contact with the students in conflict
  — Building their credibility with the students
  — Promoting rapport between the students

- Guide the mediation
  — Help the students assess the various approaches to solving the conflict
  — Help the students select an approach
- Build trust and cooperation between the students
  — Handling the emotions of the parties
  — Clarifying the communications between the students
- Help define the issues of the conflict
  — Obtaining agreement from the students to discuss the issues
  — Obtaining agreement from the students on what issues to discuss
- Help generate solutions to the conflict
  — The mediator does not generate solutions but helps the students generate solutions
- Help achieve agreement on a solution
- Help students evaluate the solution after it is in effect

Peer mediation has been successful in many schools throughout the country. Students should be taught both conflict resolution and peer mediation skills at a young age. The sooner they are taught, the more effective they will be as they get older. This outline presented may also be used to increase teacher, administrator and parent skills in conflict and mediation.

Appendix I

Anger Management Course Outline

1. Definition of anger
   - A feeling of indignation and hostility that involves complex emotions and depends on how we evaluate events and/or situations. Our own thought processes perpetuate anger
   - Everyone has angry feelings at one time or another
2. Negative functions of anger:
   - A disrupter — Makes it difficult to think clearly and evaluate options
   - An instigator — May cause a person to discharge or release feelings in an irresponsible manner
   - A conveyor — Can give a negative impression to others
3. Constructive functions of anger:
   - An energizer — It gives us vigor and stamina
   - A cue — It gives us information about people and situations
   - An expressor — We can communicate our negative feelings to other people
4. Situations at school that may cause anger:
   - Frustration
   - Stress
   - Perceived injustices
   - Low self-esteem
   - Fear
   - Hurt
   - Worry

5. Unresolved anger:
   - Symptoms of unresolved anger
     — Fatigue
     — Hypersensitivity to others
     — Isolation from others
   - Unresolved anger causes distress
6. Styles of anger:
   - The person who tries not to show anger and denies his feelings
     — This is not productive because:
       - The anger may come out as sarcasm
       - It causes distress
       - Tension may build until there is an explosion
   - The person who tries to escalate the anger:
     — Starts most sentences with "you"
     — Blames and accuses others
     — Is controlling
     — This is not productive because:
       - Frequent and intense anger has a negative effect on the body and mind
       - It frequently induces violence
       - It will destroy relationships
   - The person who expresses anger clearly and appropriately to the person who has provoked him:
     — Identifies what he feels and why
     — Gets his anger message across without abusing himself or others
7. A typical anger response from people is:
   - Ready
   - Fire
   - Aim
8. A better anger response is:
   - Ready
   - Aim
   - Fire
9. A way to solve anger:
   - Decide why you have a problem
   - Outline what responses might be
   - Visualize the consequences of your response
   - Use your response
   - Evaluate how your response was received

As with conflict resolution and peer mediation, anger classes are best when role-playing is used to demonstrate different anger styles, how to deal with them, how to respond to them, and how to deal with the student's own anger. This outline can also be used to train teachers, administrators and parents in anger management skills.

Appendix J

Stress Management Class Outline

1. Definition of stress:
   - Wear and tear on the body caused by life
2. Definition of common stress terms:
   - Stressor — Situation or event that causes stress
   - Stress reaction — Physical, emotional, or behavioral response to stressor
   - Distress — Stress that is considered detrimental
   - Eustress — Stress that is considered pleasant in the long run
   - Burnout — Not stress, but a product of stress when a student has too much distress for too long and not enough coping skills
3. General Adaptation Syndrome, per Hans Selye:
   - The alarm stage — Fight or flight response. The body sends out a biochemical messenger for a "call-to-arms"
   - The resistance stage — The body tries to return to normal
   - The exhaustion stage — The body does not have a chance to recover and stress can cause damage to some part of the body
4. Symptoms of stress:
   - Headaches
   - Backaches
   - Sleeplessness
   - Hostility
   - Anxiety

5. Type A behavior patterns:
   - Walking, talking, and eating rapidly
   - Trying to do two things at once
   - Aggressiveness
   - Feelings of hostility
   - Anger
6. Type B behavior patterns:
   - Not hurried
   - Patient with others
   - Not necessarily aggressive
7. Stress and life changes:
   - The effects that changes in one's life have on stress
8. Women and stress:
9. Long term effects of stress:
   - High blood pressure
   - Heart disease
10. Students and stress:
    - Differences in how adults and children cope with stress
11. Stress management techniques:
    - Physical exercise
    - Talk things over with others
    - Take care of yourself

Remember, the outlines for classes are only outlines and a lot of material can be used to make classes interesting and helpful for students. In stress management, it is helpful to obtain self-evaluation questionnaires to help students evaluate themselves in relation to the stress in their lives. Also, stress management classes can be useful for teachers, administrators, and parents.

Appendix K

Selecting a Safety/Security Consultant

Selecting a consultant to work with your school to help in matters of safety and security may be difficult. As with any new phenomenon, there will be people who pass themselves off to be experts and really do not have any experience or knowledge. When the standards of the International Standards Organization (ISO) became mandated for many industries, consultants came out of the woodwork to get in on the new-found wealth of helping companies become certified in ISO. Some knew what they were doing but many did not, and those that did not know what they were doing did not help organizations.

You will want to hire an individual who has experience in both safety and security and has some knowledge of school violence and gangs. There are a number of law enforcement people who have experience in security but may or may not have experience with school violence or gangs. Since mass murder in schools is relatively new, there are not a lot of experts who have credentials in this type of situation. The only experts may be the school personnel who have been through the situation. There are, however, many people who have experience with gangs and gang-related problems in schools.

When selecting a consultant, be sure to check his or her credentials to make sure he or she has the background and experience claimed. It may be wise to appoint an in-house safety and security consultant and arrange for training related to school violence, gangs, etc. An in-house person already has knowledge of the school plant and its students. It may be less expensive to train an insider than to hire an outside consultant. After being trained, the in-house consultant will be able to train all teachers and administrators in the latest safety/security measures that they can use. The in-house person can also work with school administrators on how to practice different safety procedures for the best outcomes. Large school districts may need an in-house consultant for each building. The only caution is that the person trained must be given the authority to do the things that need to be done to make the school safe and secure. In the case where the school district has its own police force, they can be responsible for training teachers and administrators in safety and security measures.

Appendix L

Resources

The following is a list of resources that you can contact if you need assistance in preventing violence in school or in preventing gang-related violence.

Antigang Organizations

National Youth Gang Information Center
Institute for Intergovernmental Research
P.O. Box 12729
Tallahassee, FL 33217
Phone (850) 385-0600
www.iir.com/nygc/

Florida Gang Investigators (for law enforcement)
2601 Blair Stone Road
Tallahassee, FL 32399-2500
Phone (850) 410-4582

Street Law Inc.
918 Sixteenth Street, NW, Suite 600
Washington, DC 20006-2902
Phone (202) 293-0088
www.streetlaw.org

Teens, Crime and the Community
1700 K Street, NW, Second Floor
Washington, DC 2006-3817
Phone (202) 466-6272, ext. 152 or 161
www.nationaaltcc.org

Gang Resistance Education and Training Program
Bureau of Alcohol, Tobacco, and Firearms
Phone (800) 726-7070

Office of Juvenile Justice and Delinquency Prevention
810 Seventh Street, NW
Washington, DC 20531
Phone (800) 638-8736
www.askncjrs @ ncjrs.org

National Institutes of Health (NIH)
Bethesda, MD 20892

School Organizations

United States Department of Education
400 Maryland Avenue, SW
Washington, DC 20202-0498
Phone (800) 872-5327

National PTA
330 North Wabash Avenue, Suite 2100
Chicago, IL 60611
Phone (800) 307-4782

National School Safety Center
4165 Thousand Oaks Blvd., Suite 296
Westlake Village, CA 91362
Phone (805) 373-9977
www.nssc.org

Center for the Study and Prevention of Violence
Institute of Behavioral Science
University of Colorado
Campus Box 442, Building 10
Boulder, CO 80309-0442
Phone (303) 492-8465
www.colorado.edu/cspu/

National Center for Conflict Resolution Education
Illinois Institute for Dispute Resolution
110 West Main Street
Urbana, IL
Phone (217) 384-4118

Kentucky Center for School Safety
Eastern Kentucky University
300 Stratton Building
521 Lancaster Avenue
Richmond, KY 40475
Phone (877) 805-4277

School Board Associations

American Association of School Administrators
1801 North Moore Street
Arlington, VA 22209
Phone (703) 528-0700
www.aasa.org

National School Board Association
1680 Duke Street
Alexandria, VA 22314
Phone (708) 838-6722
www.nsba.org/

Alabama Association of School Boards
Drawer 230488
Montgomery, AL 36123-0488

Association of Alaska School Boards
316 West 11th Street
Juneau, AK 99801-1510
Phone (907) 586-1083

Arizona School Board Association
2100 North Central Avenue
Phoenix, AZ 85004-1400
Phone (602) 254-1100

Arkansas School Board Association
808 Dr. Martin Luther King Drive
Little Rock, AR 72202-3631
Phone (501) 372-1415
www.arsba.org

California School Board Association
P.O. Box 1668
West Sacramento, CA 95691-1660
Phone (916) 371-4691
www.csba.org

Colorado Association of School Boards
1200 Grant Street
Denver, CO 80203-2306
Phone (800) 530-8430
www.casb.org

Connecticut Association of School Boards
81 Wolcott Hill Road
Wethersfield, CT 06109-1242
Phone (860) 571-7446
www.cabc.org

Delaware School Board Association
P.O. Box 1277
Dover, DE 19903-1277
Phone (302) 678-2265

Board of Education of the District of Columbia
825 North Capitol Street NW
Washington, DC 20002
Phone (202) 442-5600

Florida School Board Association
203 South Monroe Street
Tallahassee, FL 32301-1823
Phone (850) 414-2578

Georgia School Board Association
5120 Sugar Loaf Parkway
Lawrenceville, GA 30043
Phone (770) 962-2985
Phone (800) 226-1856
www.com/gsba

Idaho School Board Association
5909 W. State Street
Boise, ID 83703
Phone (208) 854-1476
www.idsba.org

Illinois Association of School Boards
4306 Vine Street
Springfield, IL 62703-22036
Phone (217) 528-9688
www.iasb.com

Indiana School Board Association
One North Capitol Avenue
Indianapolis, IN 46204-2026
Phone (317) 639-0330

Iowa Association of School Boards
700 2nd Avenue, Suite 100
Des Moines, IA 50309-1713
Phone (515) 288-1991
www.ia-sb.org

Kansas Association of School Boards
1420 SW Arrowhead Road
Topeka, KS 66604-4001
Phone (913) 273-3600

Kentucky School Board Association
260 Democrat Drive
Frankfort, KY 40601-9214
Phone (502) 695-4603
www.ksba.org

Louisiana School Board Association
7912 Summa Avenue
Baton Rouge, LA 70809-3416
Phone (225) 769-3191

Maine School Board Association
49 Community Drive
Augusta, ME 04330-9405
Phone (207) 622-3473

Maryland Association of Boards of Education
621 Ridgely Avenue, Suite 300
Annapolis, MD 21401-1087
Phone (410) 841-5414

Massachusetts Association of School Committees Inc.
One McKinney Square
Boston, MA 02109
Phone (617) 423-8454

Michigan Association of School Boards
1001 Centennial Way, Suite 400
Lansing, MI 48917
Phone (517) 327-5900

Mississippi School Board Association
P.O. Box 203
Clinton, MS 39060-0203
Phone (601) 924-2001

Missouri School Board Association
2100 1-70 Drive, SW
Columbia, MO 65203-0099
Phone (9573) 445-9920

Montana School Board Association
1 South Montana Avenue
Helena, MT 59601-5178
Phone (406) 642-2180
www.mtsba.org

Nebraska Association of School Boards
140 South 16th Street
Lincoln, NE 68508-1805
Phone (402) 475-4951

Nevada Association of School Boards
1100 Kietzke Lane, Room 212
Reno, NV 89502-2714
Phone (702) 32304828

New Hampshire School Board Association
14 Fayette Street
Concord, NH 03301-3711
Phone (603) 228-2061

New Jersey School Board Association
P.O. Box 909
Trenton, NJ 08605-0909
Phone (609) 695-7600
www.njsba.org

New Mexico School Board Association
300 Galisteo Street, Suite 204
Santa Fe, NM 87501-2606
Phone (505) 983-5041

New York State School Board Association
119 Washington Avenue
Albany, NY 12210-2204
Phone (518) 465-3474

North Carolina School Board Association
P.O. Box 97068
Raleigh, NC 28624-7068
Phone (919) 081-2630
www.ncsba.org

North Dakota School Board Association
110 North 3rd Street
Bismarck, ND 58502-2276
Phone (701) 255-4127

Ohio School Board Association
8050 North High Street
Columbus, OH 43235
Phone (614) 540-4000

Oklahoma State School Board Association
2801 North Lincoln Blvd.
Oklahoma City, OK 73105-4223
Phone (405) 528-3571

Oregon School Board Association
P. O. Box 1068
Salem, OR 97308-1068
Phone (503) 588-2800
www.osba.org

Pennsylvania School Board Association
774 Limekiln Road
New Cumberland, PA 17070-2315
Phone (717) 774-2331
www.psba.org

Rhode Island Association of School Committees
Rhode Island College Campus
Building 6
600 Mount Pleasant Avenue
Providence, RI 02908-1991
Phone (401) 272-9811

South Carolina School Board Association
1027 Barnwell Street
Columbia, SC 29201-3836
Phone (803) 799-6607

Associated School Boards of South Dakota
P. O. Box 1059
Pierre, SD 57501-1059
Phone (605) 224-6293

Tennessee School Board Association
1130 Nelson Merry Street
Nashville, TN 37203-2800
Phone (615) 741-4707

Texas Association of School Boards
P. O. Box 400
Austin, TX 78767-0400
Phone (512) 467-0222

Utah School Board Association
860 East 9085 South
Sandy, UT 84094-3064
Phone (801) 566-1277

Vermont School Board Association
2 Prospect Street
Montpelier, VT 05602-3555
Phone (802) 223-3580
Phone (800) 244-8722

Virginia School Board Association
2370-B Hunters Way
Charlottesville, VA 22911-7931

Washington State School Directors' Association
221 College Street, NE
Olympia, WA 98516-5313
Phone (360) 493-9231

West Virginia School Board Association
2206 Washington Street East
P. O. Box 1008
Charlestown, WV 24324
Phone (304) 346-0571

Wisconsin Association of School Boards
122 West Washington Avenue, Suite 400
Madison, WI 53703-2718
Phone (608) 257-2622

Wyoming School Board Association
2323 Pioneer Avenue
Cheyenne, WY 82011-3611
Phone (307) 634-1112

State Departments of Education

Alabama Department of Education
50 North Ripley Street
Montgomery, AL 36130-2101
Phone (334) 242-9700

Alaska Department of Education
801 West 10th Street, Suite 200
Juneau, AK 99801
Phone (907) 465-2800

Arizona Department of Education
1535 West Jefferson Street
Phoenix, AZ 85007
Phone (602) 542-4361
Hot Line (800) 352-4558

Arkansas Department of Education
4 Capitol Mall
Little Rock, AR 72201
Phone (501) 682-4475
www.arkedu.state.ar.us/ade.htm

California Department of Education
721 Capitol Mall
Sacramento, CA 95814

Colorado Department of Education
201 East Colfax Avenue
Denver, CO 80203

Connecticut Department of Education
P. O. Box 2219
Hartford, CT
Phone (860) 566-5677

Florida Department of Education
www.firn.edu/doe/doehome/html.

Georgia Department of Education
2066 Twin Tower East
Atlanta, GA 30334-5001
Phone (404) 656-2800
Safety hotline (877) 729-7867

Hawaii Department of Education
P. O. Box 2360
Honolulu, HI 96804

Idaho Department of Education
P. O. Box 83720
Boise, ID
Phone (208) 332-6800

Illinois Department of Education
100 North 1st Street
Springfield, IL
100 West Randolph Street
Chicago, IL

Indiana Department of Education
Room 229 State House
Indianapolis, IN 46704-2798
Voice mail (317) 232-0808

Kansas Department of Education
120 S.E. 10th Avenue
Topeka, KS 66612-1182
Phone (785) 296-3201

Kentucky Department of Education
500 Mero Street, 1st Floor
Frankfort, KY 40601
Phone (502) 546-3141

Maine Department of Education
23 State House Station
Augusta, ME 04333

Maryland Department of Education
200 West Baltimore Street
Baltimore, MD 21201
Phone (410) 767-0600
Phone (888) 246-0016

Michigan Department of Education
608 West Allegan Street
Hannah Building
Lansing, MI 48933

Mississippi State Board of Education
P. O. Box 771
Jackson, MS 39205

Montana Department of Education
P. O. Box 202501
Helena, MT 59620-2501
Phone (406) 444-3095

Nebraska Department of Education
901 Centennial Mall South
Lincoln, NE 68509-1987
Phone (402) 471-2295

Nevada Department of Education
700 East 5th Street
Carson City, NV 89701-5096
Phone (702) 687-9217

New Hampshire Department of Education
101 Pleasant Street
Concord, NH 03301-3860
Phone (603) 271-3494
Citizens' Service (800) 339-9900

New Jersey Department of Education
100 River View Executive Plaza
CN 500
Trenton, NJ 08625
Phone (609) 292-4469

South Carolina Department of Education
1429 Senate Street
Rutledge Building
Columbia, SC
Phone (803) 734-8815

South Dakota Department of Education
700 Governors Drive
Kneip Building, 3rd Floor
Pierre, SD 57501-2291

Tennessee Department of Education
Andrew Johnson Tower, 6th Floor
710 James Robertson Parkway
Nashville, TN 37243-0375
Phone (615) 740-2731

Texas Department of Education
1701 North Congress Avenue
Austin, TX 78701-1494
Phone (512) 463-9734

Utah Department of Education
250 East 500 South
Salt Lake City, UT 84111
Phone (801) 538-7500

Vermont Department of Education
120 State Street
Montpelier, VT 05620-2501
Phone (802) 828-3147

Virginia Department of Education
101 North 14th Street
James Monroe Building
Richmond, VA
Phone (800) 292-3820

Washington Department of Education
Old Capitol Building
P. O. Box 47200
Olympia, WA 98504-7200
Phone (360) 753-6738
TDD (360) 664-3631

West Virginia Department of Education
1900 Kanawha Blvd.
Charleston, WV 25305
Phone (304) 558-2681

Wisconsin Department of Education
125 South Webster Street
P. O. Box 7841
Madison, WI 53702-7841
Phone (800) 441-4563

Wyoming Department of Education
2300 Capitol Avenue
Hathaway Building, 2nd Floor
Cheyenne, WY 82002-0050

District of Columbia Department of Education
825 North Capitol Street, NE
Washington, DC 20002

References

Able, Charley, Ann Imse, and Kevin Vaughn. "Deputy Knew of Harris Threats," *Denver Rocky Mountain News*, April 30, 1994.

Berger, Gilda, *Violence and Drugs*, (Franklin Watts: New York, 1989).

Berkowitz, Leonard, *Aggression: Its Causes, Consequences, and Control*, (McGraw-Hill: New York, 1993).

Blank, Jonah, Jason Vest, and Susie Parker, "The Children of Jonesboro," *U.S. News, & World Report* (April 6, 1998).

Blank, Jonah, and Warren Blank, "Prayer Circle Murders," *U.S. News & World Report* (December 15, 1997).

Blank, Jonah, "The Kid No One Noticed," *U.S. News & World Report* October 12, 1998.

Bowles, Scott, "Shattered School Days," *USA Today*, (December 3, 1997).

Cabell, Brian, "Teen Killer Sobs as Confession is Played in Court," *CNN.com*, (June 11, 1998).

Chua-Eoan, Howard, "Mississippi Gothic," *Time*, vol. 150, no. 16, 10-20-97. (October 20, 1997).

Cloud, John, "What Can the Schools Do?" *Time*, (May 3, 1999).

Cloud, John, "Just a Routine School Shooting," *Time*, (May 31, 1999).

Corliss, Richard, "Bang, You're Dead," *Time*, (May 3, 1999).

Cozie, Charles P, *Gangs: Opposing Viewpoints*, (Greenhaven Press Inc.: San Diego, CA 1996)

Couric, Katie, "Coverage of Littleton Shooting," *The Today Show*, (April 21–23, 1998).

Cullen, Dave, "Massacre in Suburban Denver," *Salonmagazine.com*, (March 30, 1998).

Decker, Scott, H., and Barrik Van Winkle, *Life in the Gang: Family, Friends and Violence*, (Cambridge University Press: New York 1996).

Diagnostic and Statistical Manual of Mental Disorders, IV, (American Psychiatric Association: Washington, DC, 1994).

Fish, Sandra, "Tuesday's Brutal High School Slayings Come as a Shock to Many," *Boulder News*, (April 22, 1999).

Fleeman, Michael, "School Shooting Spurs Debate on Entertainment's Role in Youth Violence," *Associated Press*, (April 23, 1999).

Gest, Ted, with Victoria Pope, "Crime Time Bomb," *U.S. News Online*, (March 25, 1996).

Gibbs, Nancy, "The Littleton Massacre," *Time,* (May 3, 1999).

Grace, Julie, "When the Silence Fell," *Time,* vol. 150, no. 25, (December 15, 1997).

Hardwell, Shelia, "Teens Plead Not Guilty," *Associated Press,* (October 8, 1998).

Howlett, Debbie, "School Tries to Return to Normal," *USA Today,* (May 26, 1998).

Hazlehurst, Kayleen, and Cameron Hazlehurst, ed. *Gangs and Youths Subcultures,* (Transaction Publishers: New Brunswick & London, 1998).

Henry, Tamara, "Report Finds Drop in Violence but Rise in Gangs at School," *Boulder News,* October 15, 1998.

Hillard, Carl, "Parents of Columbine Shooters Sued," *Associated Press,* (May 28, 1999).

Humphreys, Christine, "School Shooting in Oregon," *ABC News,* (May 21, 1998).

Hornblower, Margot, "The Boy who Loved Bombs," *Time,* vol. 151, no. 21, (June 1, 1998).

James, Ian, "Shots Fired at Miami High School, 3 People Wounded," *Seattle Times,* (September 30, 1998).

Katel, Peter, "Five Killed at Arkansas School," *USA Today,* (March 25, 1996).

Kim, Henry, ed., *Youth Violence: Current Controversies,* (Greenhaven Press: San Diego, 1998).

Kim, Henry, ed., *Guns and Violence: Current Controversies,* (Greenhaven Press: San Diego, 1999).

Knox, George W. *National Gangs Resource Handbook,* (Wyndham Hall Press: Bristol, IN, 1994).

Knox, Noelle, "Spending For Safety," *ABCNews.com,* (April 29, 1998).

Landre, Rick, Mike Miller, and Dee Porter, *Gangs: A Handbook for Community Awareness,* (Facts on File Inc: New York, 1997).

Leibovich, Lori, "Making Sense of Jonesboro," *Salonmagazine.com,* (March 30, 1998).

Lobi, Nadya, "The Hunter and the Choirboy," *Time,* vol. 151, no. 13, (April 6, 1998).

Lacayo, Richard, "Toward the Root of Evil," *Time,* vol. 151, no. 13, (April 6, 1998).

Mirande, Alfredo, *Gringo Justice,* (University of Notre Dame Press: Notre Dame, IN, 1987).

Marshall, Steve, "Attack Comes with Insidious Twist," *USA Today,* (March 25, 1998).

Megargee, E., "The Prediction of Dangerous Behavior," *Criminal Justice and Behavior,* vol. 3, (1976).

Monahan, John, "Dangerous and Violent Behavior," *Journal of Occupational Medicine,* (October–December, 1986).

Monahan, John, "Mental Disorder and Violent Behavior," *American Psychologist,* (April 1992).

Monahan, John, "The Cause of Violence," *FBI Law Enforcement Bulletin* (January 1994).

Monahan, John, *Predicting Violent Behavior: An Assessment of Clinical Techniques,* (Sage Publication Beverly Hills, CA, 1981).

Moore, Jack B. *Skinheads Shaved for Battle: A Cultural History of American Skinheads,* (Bowling Green University Popular Press: Bowling Green, OH, 1993).

Morello, Carol, "Woodham Gets Life: Motive May Never be Known," *USA Today,* (June 15, 1998).

National Association of Attorneys General, School Search Reference Guide, (1999).

National School Safety Center, Student Searches and the Law: An Administrator's Guide to Conducting Legal Searches on School Campuses, (1995).

"Anatomy of a Massacre," *Newsweek,* (May 3, 1999).

Okrent, Daniel, "Raising Kids Online," *Time,* (May 10, 1999).

O'Neill, Patrick, "Experts: Inner Chaos Fuels Kids Who Kill," *The Oregonian,* (May 25, 1998).

"One Slain Five Critical at Oregon High School," *Seattle Times,* (May 21, 1998).

Pooley, Eric, "Portrait of a Deadly Bond," *Time,* (May).

Popyk, Lisa, "Blood in the Schoolyard," *Cincinnati Post,* (November 7, 9, and 11, 1998).

Preventing and Coping with School Violence: A Resource Manual for Indiana School Employees, (Indiana State Teachers Association, Indianapolis, IN, 1998).

Richardson, Gwen Day, "Kentucky Attack a Sign of Growing Violence," *USA Today,* (December 5, 1997).

Ritter, John, and Marty Kasindorf, "Nobody Took Him Seriously," *USA Today,* (May 22, 1998).

Rogers, Adam, Pat Wingert, and Thomas Hayden, "Why the Young Kill," *Newsweek,* (May 3, 1999).

Serrano, Barbara, "How Can We Know Our Schools are Safe?" *Seattle Times,* (May 5, 1999).

Sharp, Deborah, "Student Gun Violence Creeps into Small Community Schools," *USA Today,* (December 3, 1997).

Silverstein, Herma, *Kids Who Kill,* (Twenty-First Century Books: New York, 1997).

Streisand, Betsy, and Angie Cannon, "Exorcising the Pain," *U.S. News & World Report,* (May 10, 1998).

Temple, Linda, "School Harassment has Outgrown Playground Bullying," *USA Today,* (October 20, 1998).

The American Heritage Dictionary, (Houghton Mifflin Co.: Boston, 1989).

Tizin, Alex, "Scarred by Killings, Moses Lake Asks What has this Town Become," *Seattle Times,* (February 23, 1997).

Tizin, Alex, "Town Puzzles over 'Virus' of Youth Violence," *Seattle Times,* (February 6, 1996).

Toch, Hans, and Kenneth Adams, *The Disturbed Violent Offender,* (Yale University Press New Haven and London, 1989).

Van Dyke, Jon M, and Melvin M. Sakurai, *Checklists for Searches and Seizures in Public Schools,* (1999).

Wiggins, James A., Beverly B. Wiggins and James Vander Zanden, *Social Psychology: Fifth Edition,* (McGraw-Hill: New York, 1994).

Witkin, Gordon, Mike Tharp, Joanne M. Schrof, Thomas Toch, and Christy Scattarella, "Again," *U.S. News & World Report* (June 1, 1998).

Witkin, Gordon, "Anti-Violence Efforts Show Few Results," *U.S. News & World Report* (June 6, 1998).

Woodward, Steve, "Good Times, Bad Tempers: What Gives?" *The Oregonian,* (May 24, 1998).

www.bouldernew.com/shooting/4251927.html

www.cdc.gov/od/oc/media/fact/violenc.

www.colorado.edu/cspv/

Index